D1745901

GUIDE TO MODERN ARCHITECTURE

Reyner Banham

GUIDE TO MODERN ARCHITECTURE

The Architectural Press, London

By the same author

THEORY AND DESIGN IN THE FIRST MACHINE AGE

© ARCHITECTURAL PRESS, 1962

Printed in Great Britain by
WILLMER BROTHERS AND HARAM LTD, BIRKENHEAD

CONTENTS

The chapters are accompanied by marginal illustrations

Acknowledgements 7

Introduction 9

1. **MODERN** 13

2. **FUNCTION** 21

3. **FORM** 30

4. **CONSTRUCTION** 38

5. **SPACE** 45

Index 157

ILLUSTRATIONS

The illustrations are accompanied by a textual commentary

Flats on the Zaanstraat, Amsterdam, Michel de Klerk 53
The Schröder House, Utrecht, Gerrit T. Rietveld 56
Flats in St James's Place, London, Denys Lasdun 58
Factory at Bryn Mawr, Wales, Architects' Co-Partnership 62
Factory at Blumberg, Germany, Egon Eiermann, 62
The Ford House, Aurora, Illinois, Bruce Goff 64
Penguin Pool, London Zoo, Lubetkin and Tecton 68
Town Hall, Kurashiki, Japan, Kenzo Tange 70
Laboratories in Philadelphia, Louis Kahn 72
Como, Works of Giuseppe Terragni 76
Casa del Girasole, Rome, Luigi Moretti 80
House on the Zattere, Venice, Ignazio Gardella 80
The Robie House, Chicago, Frank Lloyd Wright 82
Schocken Store, Stuttgart, Eric Mendelsohn 84
Johnson Wax Company Buildings, Racine, Wisconsin, Frank Lloyd Wright 88
Unité d'Habitation, Marseilles, Le Corbusier 92
The Seagram Building, New York, Philip Johnson and Mies van der Rohe 96
Lever House, New York, Gordon Bunshaft of Skidmore, Owings and Merrill 96
Pirelli Tower, Milan, Gio Ponti and associates, Pierluigi Nervi and associates 100
Termini Station, Rome, Eugenio Montuori and associates 104
Pavillon Suisse, Cité Universitaire, Paris, Le Corbusier 108
General Motors Technical and Research Centre, Warren, Michigan, Eero Saarinen and associates 112

Airport Buildings, Gatwick, Yorke, Rosenberg and
    Mardall 116
The Climatron, St Louis, Missouri, Murphy and
    Mackey 118
Harumi apartment block, Tokyo, Kunio
    Maekawa 122
Church at Imatra, Finland, Alvar Aalto, 124
Highpoint I and Highpoint II, Highgate, London,
    Lubetkin and Tecton 128
Park Hill, Sheffield, J. L. Womersley 132
Brasilia, Brazil, Oscar Niemeyer, Lucio Costa and
    others 136
Chandigarh, East Punjab, Le Corbusier 136
C.L.A.S.P. School, Milan, Nottingham County
    Architect's Department 142
The Bauhaus, Dessau, Walter Gropius 146
Crown Hall, Chicago, Mies van der Rohe 150

ACKNOWLEDGEMENTS

Acknowledgements are due for the illustrations on the following pages: Aerofilms 119 top; Annan, Glasgow 14 left; *Architects' Journal* (Sam Lambert) 59 bottom left, (John Pantlin) 117; Architectural Association 39, 55 top; *Architectural Forum* 65; *Architectural Review* (de Burgh Galwey) 27 centre, 132, 135, (W. J. Toomey) 133, (Dell and Wainwright) 50 bottom, 129, 131 both; Archives Photographiques, Paris, 38 right; Banham, arphot 43 bottom and centre right; Behr photography 59 top, 61; Jean Bouvry 44; Bryan and Shear Ltd. 14 right; Foto A. Cartoni 80, 81 top; *Casabella* 125; Foto-Studio Casali 81 bottom; Cement and Concrete Association 43 top right; Chevojon, Paris 31 bottom; Chicago Heritage Committee 42 top; Peter Collins and Faber and Faber 42 bottom; David Crease 139; Crown copyright 143, 145; Doeser Fotos, Laren 57; Dyckerhoff and Widmann Archiv, Munich 43 top centre; Charles Eames 28 top, 64 both; Bill Engdahl, Hedrich-Blessing 154, 155; Y. Futagawa 122, 123; Marcel Gautherot 139 top, 140; Gemeentelijke Woningsdienst 55 top; General Motors Corporation 115 top; Editions Girsberger 26, 35, 93, 109, 111; Heikki Havas 127 bottom; John Havinden 68, 69; Hedrich-Blessing, Chicago, 49, 50 top two, 121, 151, 153; Lucien Hervé 25 both, 43 top left, 95 all three, 113 top; John Hillelson Agency (Brian Brake) 141 top; Ch. Hirayama 71; Jurgen Joedicke 32 centre; Philip Johnson and the Museum of Modern Art, New York 34 bottom two; S. C. Johnson & Son, 89 bottom left and right; Keystone Press Agency 88; G. E. Kidder Smith 36 both, 77 bottom, 107 both; H. Lacheroy 51 bottom, 52; J. Alex Langley 99; Franz Lazi Junior 63 bottom; Roger Mayne 134 all three, 136; Millar and Harris 48 top left and right; *Milwaukee Journal* photo 89 top; Lucia Moholy-Nagy 147 bottom, 149; Museo Civico, Como 33; Paul Popper Ltd 51 top; Publifoto, Milan, 147 top; Rijksvoorlichtingsdienst 85 bottom; Cervin Robinson 75 both, 97, (Arphot U.S.) 101 top; H. Roger-Viollet 38 left; Alberto Sartoris and the R.I.B.A. Library, 78, 79 both; Aaron Siskind and Richard Nickel (courtesy *Architectural Forum*) 83, 85 top; James Stirling 27 top; Ezra Stoller 37, 91, 101 bottom, 113 bottom;

H. Tempest (Cardiff) Ltd. 63 top; Toshio Taira 73; United States Information Service 48 bottom left and right; Giulia Veronesi and Libreria Editrice Tamburini 77; Foto Welin 127 top; Valerie Winter 141 bottom; Zumstein, Bern, 41 top left.

INTRODUCTION

We architecture fans get a poor look-in when modern architecture is being discussed. All too quickly, the discussion becomes a tussle between producers and consumers: the producers—architects—make high-level utterances meant only to be understood by other architects, and occasionally condescend to issue broadsheets and primers to the hoi-polloi; the latter write one another resentful newspaper articles about the horrors of modern architecture.

But what about buffs like myself who genuinely enjoy modern architecture and get real pleasure from looking at modern buildings; will even go out of our ways, or reorganise a holiday for the sake of the sight of a work by Mies van der Rohe, le Corbusier or even lesser lights? We have been atrociously badly served: the literature of appreciation is very thin. We are allowed to bow down in loutish adoration of the attempts that modern architects have made to improve our miserable lot; we are encouraged to gawp at the private lives and non-architectural activities of a man like Frank Lloyd Wright. But we are not encouraged to cheer and stamp when a Gio Ponti successfully pulls off a rather *risqué* aesthetic effect, when le Corbusier transmutes the flatulence of three hundred flats into a rhetorical exhaust stack in the grandest of all possible manners, or when Mies turns the corner of a façade with the authority and precision of Fangio at Woodcote.

We want to know when to applaud; to give expression to our relish of a smart piece of professionalism, some sustained design-logic, an aesthetic opportunity seized, a known theme radically re-worked in a manner that would have the Sunday papers raving, had it been by Anouilh or Stravinsky. The mere fact that, at this point, one has to turn to other arts for a handy comparison, is a fair measure of the way in which architectural appreciation has been beaten down by the glass-eyed solemnity of the Ruskin tradition, and diluted to tastelessness by the mincing frivolity of the followers of Geoffrey Scott.

There ought to be pieces of architectural skill or bravura that are as familiar to the cultivated eye as Picasso's combined full-face/profiles, sustained passages of close-knit invention as commonly explored as the Alexandria Quartet. Yet nothing such springs to mind: modern architecture has been murdered by its apologists, so careful to prevent its misrepresentation that they failed to represent it as anything but an unlovable and unlovely moral example.

This complaint is not new, but the present time seems a good one to try and remedy the situation. There is a lot of modern architecture about nowadays, it has greater variety than it had before, and its greatest practitioners, having reached the age of mastery, have endowed it with an authority that was not reliably there before. Modern architecture can nourish a body of fans and fanciers, much as any other period of architecture can . . . more than any other period can, because its monuments are imbued with an immediacy that even the masterpieces of the Victorians have lost. All the buildings described in the pages that follow have struck me hard, personally, with a power and authority that derives from their being the results of creative acts done in our time, by men subject to the same pressures, distractions and enthusiasms as myself.

I have therefore discussed them as monuments to the creative skill of men in a particular situation—our present situation—not as demonstrations of philosophy or justifications of any theory. However, it is characteristic of creative men that their heads perpetually buzz with philosophies, ideas, ideals, theories and verbal formulae and slogans and social aspirations, many of which are now seen to be fallible in logic or fact. Nevertheless, they have not proven fallible as sources of inspiration, and they, too, therefore deserve to be discussed—but not as the revealed word of Truth, as was the custom of the thirties. Ideas and theories of modern architecture have been warped, discarded, inverted, misrepresented—few stand unaltered from the days of their creation. Yet, in their mutability is their strength—the surest way to show you have a mind is to change it, and the changing mind of modern architecture is proof of its growing maturity, just as the buildings themselves are the monuments of its growing authority.

1. MODERN

> Whatever happened to that old modern
> architecture?   Edward D. Stone

The fact that we can now speak of modern architecture as 'mature' or grown up, is a sure sign that when the word *modern* is used in this context, it no longer means what it used to mean. If something has had time to mature it cannot possess the bang-up-to-date, born-yesterday, as-of-now, attributes that used to be covered by modern; what the word means here is *not old*, the division between the new and the old being as fixed as that between the Old and New Testaments, B C and A D.

For the art of painting, the date that divides the new from the old is tacitly allowed to be somewhere in the Impressionist period, around 1870. For architecture it is somewhere around 1900, in the period of the style known as Art Nouveau. Whether one takes Art Nouveau to be the last of the old-fashioned styles, or the first of the new-fangled ones, it can be agreed that this period represents the division between new and old, because most of the attributes of the new, or modern architecture, appeared during the bare fifteen turbulent years in which the style flourished, even if no building of the period quite warrants the label modern.

The School of Art in Glasgow, designed on both sides of 1900 by Charles Rennie Mackintosh, is a case in point. In practically every aspect, the manner of building balances uneasily between old and new, one thing leaning a little towards the old, something else balancing it out by inclining toward the purely modern. Its materials—masonry, brick, wood and wrought iron—are not modern, nor is the continual reliance on handicraft techniques and applied decoration. Yet the kind of building that Mackintosh made out of these materials and methods is, in some crucial aspects, unmistakably modern. In almost every part it is honest

Charles Rennie Mackintosh, 1868-1928, was the last British architect of undoubted genius. His creative career effectively spanned the last decade of the nineteenth century and the first decade of our own; his best work was all in and around the city of Glasgow, where the citizens have permitted a few small samples to remain. Understandably, he died in exile in England.

to the point of brutal frankness in its use of materials; the construction is not disguised: at the most the brick is painted over, the woodwork stained, but only walls that will need a lot of upkeep are plastered and gloss-painted so that one cannot see whether they are brick or masonry underneath, and the masonry does not conceal a steel frame.

About the way the structure works, there is a similar frankness, but it is made demonstrative: as with many modernists after him, so with Mackintosh, structure must not only be done, it must manifestly be seen to be done. A row of brick arches, massive as those in a mediaeval crypt, erupt on the very top floor of the building, kingposts in roof-trusses are often of exaggerated

Left: library, Glasgow School of Art.
Right: exterior.

dimensions, and when a beam has to meet a post, rather than spoil beautiful timbers by notching them and concealing their mutual support, he twins the beam, and takes each half of it past the post, which is gripped between the two halves. Such solicitude for the visual identity of each member in a building is a persistent theme in modern architecture.

But out of these respectfully treated structural units Mackintosh creates—wherever he has room and opportunity—a kind of interior space that is undeniably modern; the uprights and horizontals define space without enclosing it, much as a pencil line can frame an area of paper without colouring it. In the justly-celebrated library of the Glasgow school, with its upper gallery supported on beams that do not meet the upright posts until they have gone a foot or more beyond the balustrade, the parts are not modern in themselves, being often elaborately decorated with handicraft techniques, but their interlace in space offers the beholder a type of architectural experience that is unique to the modern movement.

But the decoration, to say it again, is not modern. It is Art Nouveau at its most intensely period, most hypersensitive and most neurotically overworked. It is tolerable today because it is an expression of Mackintosh's intensely period, sensitive and neurotic personality—in some ways he must be compared to Aubrey Beardsley—and because it was conceived by him integrally with the building. If one peeled off the ornament, the bare structure would not be modern architecture but just a lifeless hulk. The Glasgow School is not modern in parts: it is in every part transitional, poised on the threshold of the modern movement.

But it has another claim on the esteem of modern architects. Mackintosh is numbered among the Pioneers of the Modern Movement, as Professor Pevsner termed them in the title of the first edition of the book in which he traced what is, in many ways, an apostolic succession from the great architectural moralists of the mid-nineteenth century, John Ruskin, Viollet-le-Duc and Gottfried Semper. This apostolic succession, the conscious handing-on of the message of a reformed attitude to design, is of vital importance to the concept of modern architecture: if only because there are times and places where modern architecture cannot be defined except as 'what is done by modern architects'

First published in 1936; new editions (as *Pioneers of Modern Design*) in 1949 and 1960. A small but immensely influential book that has established, more or less definitively, who is, or is not, a founding father of Modern Architecture. Available as a Pelican, required reading.

15

and because the modern movement can always be more rigorously defined by naming its members than by attempting to list its methods.

There is no point in formally setting out a family tree at this juncture: indeed, such graphic devices always involve falsification because of the way in which the same man can influence succeeding generations of followers in opposing directions (as Le Corbusier has done), or the way in which men on opposite sides of the world can keep in touch nowadays without ever meeting one another. But one can indicate the kind of process, the type of relationship by which the apostolic succession was built up. Three of the greatest masters of modern architecture, though born in different places and differing circumstances, studied under the same master and underwent the same influences for a short but vital part of their formative years: Walter Gropius, Mies van der Rohe and Charles Edouard Jeanneret (who later called himself Le Corbusier) all passed through the office of Peter Behrens as assistants around 1910. Behrens, at that moment, was the hero of progressive German architecture, responsible for the design of everything from factories to sales literature produced by the giant A E G combine; from him these three earnest young men imbibed the doctrine of the architect as universal designer. From the man behind Behrens, the theorist and design-politician Hermann Muthesius, they all seem to have imbibed that faith in the virtues of standardisation that Muthesius pronounced in a lecture given in 1911, and from publications and an exhibition of the epoch in Berlin they acquired an admiration for Frank Lloyd Wright, whose early houses in the Chicago suburbs indicated to them a way out of the transitional condition, which Mackintosh and Behrens never found.

In a movement as small as the modern one then was, this meant that the leadership of that generation in France and Germany, the two key countries, shared many points of common doctrine. And the movement really was small; when Madame de

Wright's influence in Europe has been devious. Before 1914 he was independently 'discovered' at least three times. By C. R. Ashbee, on behalf of the English Arts and Crafts movement; by Kuno Francke, on behalf of the higher German aestheticism; and by H. P. Berlage, the father of modern architecture in Holland. Berlage probably came closest to understanding him, but each only presented a preferred segment of Wright's fertile output to his readers or hearers. From there on it was creative misrepresentation all the way.

Mandrot, under Le Corbusier's guidance, gathered them together at la Sarraz in Switzerland for the first of the Congrès Internationale d'Architecture Moderne, the result was no mass rally; the modern movement in Europe was barely three dozen men. C I A M retained this atmosphere until well after World War I I; the leaders of modern architecture all round the globe were on christian-name terms with one another, and when they met at Bridgewater in 1947, they could still be packed into a couple of buses for an afternoon at Glastonbury Fair.

By then, C I A M was really an élite within the movement, but students flocked from all over the world to congresses like that at Aix-en-Provence to sit at the feet of the masters: the sense of an apostolic succession by personal contact remained. But, also by then, there were all over the world competent modernists no longer sufficiently aware of being reformers to want to join an organisation like C I A M. Modern architecture had matured, become accepted, was the norm—if it isn't modern nowadays, it isn't architecture any more, but archaeology, cowardice or fancy dress. Governments, both East and West, after forty years of trying to hammer modern into the ground, now build modern as a matter of pride, an assertion of progressive status. As a result, the band of dangerous radicals who rallied to la Sarraz are now, in their seventies, an establishment of elder statesmen and retired generals, titular heads of a world-wide empire now so self-sustaining that it is hardly conscious of being an empire, yet every inch of it was captured and colonised by them between 1910 and 1930.

In that heroic age, they created modern architecture with their own hands, and in the next twenty years they, and their direct followers, took it to all the world: Le Corbusier to Latin America, his pupils to Japan, Gropius to England and America, his students and followers to the Commonwealth, where they met Corbusians coming round from the other side. But when they had conquered the world, nothing was ever quite the same again.

B

The remark of Ed Stone's quoted at the head of this chapter is both wistful and defiant; wistful in remembering the grand old pioneering days when he and Buckminster Fuller were the terrors of Greenwich Village; defiant because he clearly senses that the pure white image of a new architecture that he revealed to Americans in the design of the Museum of Modern Art has become a threat, a whited sepulchre in which modern architecture could die.

But, it cannot be too emphatically said, the style that Stone set out to replace or abolish with such designs as his elegant embassy in New Delhi was only a style, it was not modern architecture, whatever he himself may have thought. Many critics and architects in the 1950s went round, like Stone, announcing with gloomy good cheer that modern architecture was dead, and drawing the wrong conclusions. All that had happened, in fact, was that modern architecture had ceased to be a stylistic teen-ager, and its practitioners were no longer compelled to wear the uniform of their peer-group for fear of expulsion from the gang, demotion from christian-name status at C I A M. Any discussion of modern architecture must concern itself largely with this period of almost paranoid teenage conformity, when walls were white, windows large, roofs flat, *or else*, just as any biography of someone in his twenties will be somewhat preoccupied with his teens. But the teen-age uniform of modern architecture, the so-called International Style, or White Architecture, nowhere near exhausts the possibilities inherent in its heredity and formation. The next move was not, as many people thought around 1950, simply to put the clock back half a century and write off modern as a mistake; there was no need to go back to the old architecture that was before 1900.

Paradoxically, the leading modernists never felt that they had really strayed from that old architecture anyhow. Not from its true and eternal principles. It should be remembered that the most famous book ever written by a modern architect is only called, in English, *Towards a New Architecture*. When Le Corbusier first launched it on the world, its title was, quite simply *Vers une Architecture*—towards an architecture, and the qualities of that architecture were established by confronting the technology of the First Machine Age with the architecture of Ancient Greece: the Parthenon, a 1921 Delage and the proposition 'This is how Phidias felt'.

Now it is difficult not to read such an argument in the sense implied by the book's English title: that an architecture that really matched up to modern technology would have to be radically different from any architecture that had gone before. But Le Corbusier's point is not that: what he wants to say is that all the great styles of the past have been the equals of their contemporary technologies, and that when our own architecture matches our own technology then we shall have an architecture as good as the Parthenon. But also—a point that he has made more of in later books—however modern and technological an architecture may be, it still has to house and shelter a race of men who have only grown a few inches taller since pre-history and only a little more intelligent, battling a force of gravity that is substantially the same on the high plains of Tibet or in the depths of Death Valley, drinking water that is still H_2O whether it comes from a spring or a tap, and breathing air that is almost as consistent in composition all over the world. And such an architecture will be viewed and judged by eyes and brains that do not differ significantly from those that looked upon Stonehenge and wondered if that kind of architecture was here to stay.

Eyes that have been trained to look on the Parthenon and Gothic cathedrals will have no real difficulty in looking at modern architecture—particularly since Doric geometrical purity and Gothic structural frankness are continually set up as standards of architectural merit by modern architects. Briefly, modern architecture is like any other architecture only more so:

Although the title misses the whole point of the book, Frederick Etchell's translation of *Vers une Architecture* into English did more than any other literary work to transmit the emotional content of modern architecture to the Anglo-Saxon world. P. Morton Shand's translation of *The New Architecture and the Bauhaus* did the same for its moral content. Both still in print, both recommended reading.

19

it has more things to say and more ways of saying them. If it has given up certain time-honoured visual comforts, such as naturalistic decoration, it is only in order to have its hands free for other things, but it is still basically what it was—functionally, the creation of fit environments for human activities, aesthetically, the creation of sculpture big enough to walk about inside. Great architecture of any period has blended the aesthetic and the functional into an indissoluble artefact where they are inseparable and indistinguishable. This was true of a simple shed like the Parthenon or a complex structure like Rheims cathedral, it was true of a complex structure like the Glasgow School of Art and it is true of a simple shed like the Climatron in St Louis.

The justification of modern architecture, and of this book, is that the methods and materials for achieving that synthesis or integration of the aims of a building are new, unlike those of any other period and specific to our own time. Just what is new and specific is not always easy to define, and modern architects themselves have been in several minds on the subject: none of the old slogans like 'form follows function' or 'truth to materials' will really serve nowadays, and attention shifts constantly from new functions to new methods of construction, from new forms to new concepts of space. None of these four considerations is in itself sufficient to explain what is new and good about modern architecture, but by illuminating the subject from each of these points in turn—Function, Form, Construction and Space—we should at least equip ourselves with enough insight, of various kinds, to penetrate some way into the essential virtue of any modern building worthy of the name.

2. FUNCTION

> The new architecture is functional: that is it is developed out of an accurate setting forth of practical demands. . . .
> Theo van Doesburg

For nearly twenty years, modern architecture was explained as if its forms were absolutely decided by the functions they had to fulfil, and the total form of its buildings by their total register of functions—and this in spite of the fact that most of its great masters had insisted that Functionalism was not enough. Nevertheless, one of the leading justifications for having a new architecture was that new functions had arisen, and old ones had changed. The reader may judge for himself how real was this justification, by trying to enumerate just how many new functions had appeared between the death of Julius Caesar and the invention of the steam engine. The monastery, the church . . . the list is so short, so few new functions had appeared that, in the Renaissance, architecture was able to resume the classical dress of Roman times with only a little letting out of seams and moving of buttons.

But with the appearance of even primitive factories, the old architectural garments began to get badly stretched; with the emergence of the railway station, the reformed prison, the elementary school, the Florence Nightingale type of hospital, the elevator office block, the grand hotel, architects were faced with functional problems for which the past was no guide: a grand hotel is not like the hospice of a monastery, it is not even a cross between a hospice and a palace; an office block is not like the scriptorium of a cathedral, it is not even like a cross between a scriptorium and a prison (whatever humorists of the nineteenth century may have implied); not even in combinations and permutations would the old solutions serve. Even while old building materials and old styles of ornament were employed, the new functions compelled the architects of the Steam Age to build in shapes and sizes that the ancients could not have recognised. Without a workable philosophy that integrated aesthetics and function, Victorian architects—save only a few of genius—failed to make convincing architecture out of their buildings, but they did not fail as disastrously as some functionalist propagandists have maintained. As has been said, what is important is not that they failed, but that they so nearly succeeded.

All the same, they didn't succeed, and what made their failure intolerable to those who had to follow them was that, by the time the twentieth century was old enough to be aware of itself, the old functions were also in transformation. For the first time in two thousand, perhaps four thousand, years, the daily life of western man (and western woman even more so) was being revolutionised. We are only just beginning to realise how profound a revolution it was that overtook domestic life in the Edwardian age, first at the top of the social order, later spreading to other levels in a process that is not yet finished. Architects, directly involved in the processes of daily domesticity, were forced to recognise the results of this revolution earlier than most of the professions or intelligentsia; a suburban house for a motorised family whose numbers are regulated by parental choice, rather than supernatural accident; the servantless house where mother may be a doctor who receives patients for psychiatric consultations; the electric house with radio, telephone, vacuum cleaner, refrigerator and all the rest of it—the house is not what it was, even before the architect has got his hands on it.

It became necessary for architects to reconsider and re-assess the basic theme of their art, the dwelling of Man. Le Corbusier's slogan 'the house—a machine to live in', is a fair measure of how radical that re-assessment could be. Indeed, the machine/house slogan is so radical that it has been much misunderstood, and much misquoted—usually on purpose. What Le Corbusier really meant was two things: one was a house that resembled a machine in being cheap, standardised, well-equipped and easily serviced, like a mass-produced car; *la maison Citrohan* he called it in an admitted pun on the French baby-car of the period. But he also meant a house that resembled a machine in being radically well suited to the needs it had to serve, designed with honest—even inspired—rationalism, but without inherited prejudices.

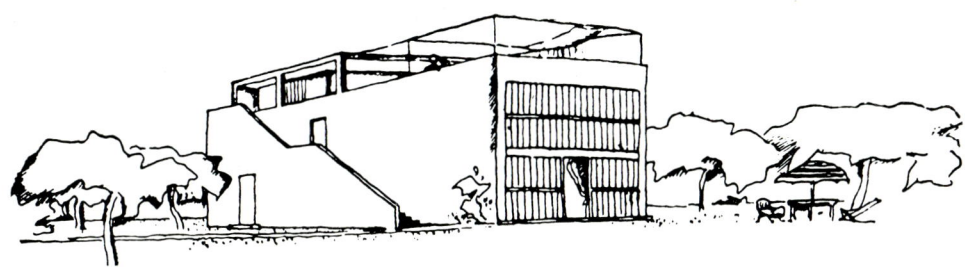

The exigencies of the twenties cheated him of the fulfilment of the mass-production dream, but he had his successes on the other side, designing, and sometimes building, a series of houses that were such radical good fits on their inhabitants that it is almost impossible for later, more tradition-bound tenants to live in them. Yet, at least one of these houses has become a Modern-Movement classic, and established something of a new norm for domestic architecture. Characteristically it is in the far suburbs of a capital city, at Poissy, down the Seine from Paris. The house does not see the river, but stands above it in a kind of ideal domestic landscape, a great square of tall grass almost entirely walled in by tall trees (that, at least, is how it was when the house was built: the chances of war and time have wrought miserably with it). Instead of invading, excavating or otherwise monumentalising this perfect setting, the house appears to touch it as little and as lightly as possible, like a helicopter poised for departure. This light stand on the ground is what, typically,

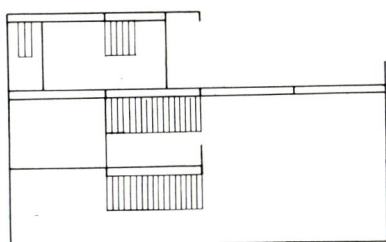

Maison Citrohan: sketch of project and, below: section showing two-storey *salon*, with sleeping-balcony at back.

23

distinguishes a modern building from an old one. In many of Richard Wilson's landscape paintings of the eighteenth century we see Palladian houses standing in equally ideal landscapes of uninterrupted lawns framed in trees, but whereas the average English stately home stood broad and heavy on its rusticated basement, Le Corbusier's Villa Savoie at Poissy stands narrow on a few slim columns.

Appears to stand . . . there is quite a lot of house on the ground floor, but it stands well back from the column line and is painted a dark colour so that it tends to disappear. But this is not just an optical trick; between the columns and the ground floor wall, under the square first floor, runs the drive, which—in the original version of the design—came from the main road, turned under the house like a race-track (the curve is preserved in the plan) and then returned, parallel to the run-in, back to the road. Thus, the house began by acknowledging that access by car was the foundation of its existence.

From drive level you ascend by a ramp—which puts the various floors in a different relationship to that implied by a staircase—to the main living floor. Although the ramp rises through the centre of the building, this floor is not, like the *piano nobile* in a comparable villa of an earlier epoch, laid out symmetrically around it. The rooms are arranged round two sides of an open court, and the ramp rises again on one side of the court to reach the roof, as in some Mediterranean peasant houses. All this complicated planning takes place within a regular square box of walls, which tell one nothing about the secret life of the house inside, except that the narrow strip of viewing window that runs all round the house is not glazed when it has open courtyard behind it. The living room, which occupies three-quarters of one side of the box and a quarter of the next, opens on to the internal court by way of a floor-to-ceiling window that forms one complete wall of the court, so that the eye travels without interruption from the carpeted floor within to the flagged floor without, even

when the sliding window is closed. There is a visual and functional ambiguity between what is certainly indoors and what is certainly out, reflecting, no doubt, the indoor/outdoor ambiguity of the daily routine of a fashionably sun-loving family of the period, and sun-bathing as such receives magnificently its due in the sun-deck on the floor above, sheltered by a loop of walls that make shapes like those in Le Corbusier's paintings, and pierced by a picture-window (the first ever) that frames a scene like a Claude or a Poussin.

This house could not have been built without twentieth-century techniques of construction, glass-making, etc., but that is not the point. There would have been no *need* to build it without the twentieth-century revolution in domestic life, and it is of crucial importance to an understanding of modern architecture to see how modern architects have shaped up to this revolution that began at home. Basically, they are still serving the same old men as have existed since Neanderthal times, more or less, still breeding, eating, secreting, excreting, sleeping, speaking, hearing, seeing much as they ever did, powered by the same old metabolisms, running at the same old pulse rates.

This familiar old Adam has occasionally been overlooked by

Top left: first-floor courtyard of Villa Savoie; right, exterior; below, plans.

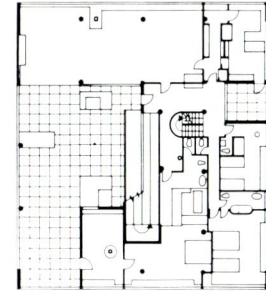
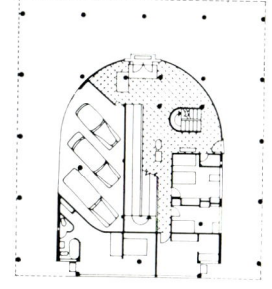

architects dizzified and dazzled by advances in technology, but not for long. Le Corbusier always has some concept of man pencilled into the corner of his drawings—his *Modulor* system of

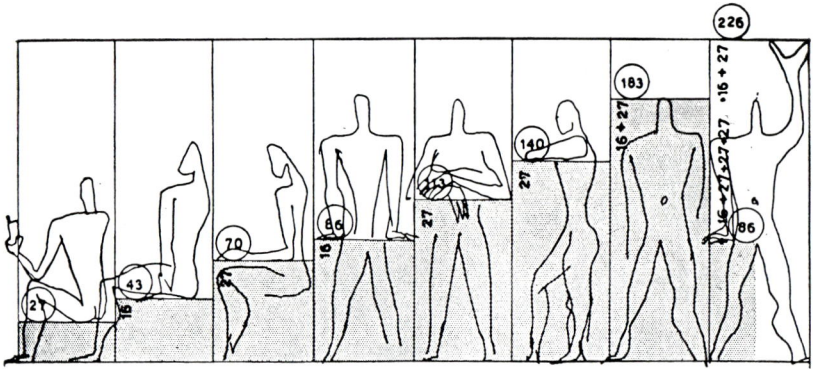

Le Corbusier's Modulor dimensions.

dimensions was based on the figure of an ideal man—and that most determined of Machine Age enthusiasts, Laszlo Moholy-Nagy, the Bauhaus philosopher, would sternly remind his readers that 'Man, not the product, is the end in view' and insist on 'the biological as the guide in everything'. This latter phrase is the key to what has really changed in the modern architect's view of function and how to design for it.

It may be the same old man, but seen in a changed new light. Moholy's 'biological' is only one of the new aspects of man as he is viewed by sociologists, doctors, psychologists, political theorists, market-researchers, traffic engineers, insurance actuaries, educators, entertainers, city-planners, economists, and everybody else who has any interest at all in making a working estimate of the capacity, needs and performance of *homo sap*. The 'man' of the older cultures was viewed *sub specie aeternitatis*, a tarnished ideal or fallen angel; the man of the culture in which architects have perforce to work nowadays must also be regarded as an observed and annotated man, a sophisticated natural man

Laszlo Moholy-Nagy has been described as the Johnny Appleseed of modern design, scattering the good word far and wide over Europe and North America. His two seed catalogues are: *The New Vision*, written in 1928 at the end of his Bauhaus years, and *Vision in Motion*, culled from the fruits of his American planting. Exhausted, he burned out and died in 1946, aged fifty-one.

who knows how he rates and can view himself through the scientific eyes of an increasingly technological culture.

Under this double aspect, we can now consider even the design of a functional church. During the teenage period of modern architecture, this would have meant a glass box with an altar at one end, and one or two such were actually built. Yet this is really only a Functional*ist* church, imitating the forms of other, obviously functional buildings such as factories. But nowadays we should mean a building that started from a rigorous analysis of the ritual to be enacted in it, its needs in terms of space, lighting, sight lines and other forms of human contact required by the religion or sect that was to use it, plus processional and other types of access and circulation within or through the 'liturgical room'. It would be the architect's task to work this out from first principles and not accept the habit-bound opinions of priest and congregation, and having found out, to reconcile all these— probably conflicting—requirements in a convincing building. The result is no more likely to be a glass box than it is to be a Romanesque crypt, and the outcome has already been as various as the bulging sail-like curves of Le Corbusier's pilgrimage chapel at Ronchamp, or the hard-edged brick and concrete angles of Robert Maguire's parish church of Saint Paul, Bow Common.

The essence of the matter seems to be that all functional problems are equal in the eyes of a good modern architect, none are too ancient nor too sacred to be re-examined, none are too trivial or too recherché to be assessed. Surprisingly few of the great modern buildings are dedicated entirely to utterly unprecedented functions, few of the entirely new functions have yet evoked first-rate architecture: where is your masterpiece among atomic power-stations? There isn't one, and this may well be due to the fact that in fields like atomics and rocketry the architect is not allowed to make a radical scrutiny of the problem because some of the information he needs is 'classified'. It is when they have been

Top: pilgrimage chapel at Ronchamp.
Bottom: parish church of St Paul, Bow Common, London.

The truly functional church is the theme of Peter Hammond's famous book *Liturgy and Architecture*, published in 1960, in nice time to provide some solid fuel for the controversies over St Paul's, Bow Common.

27

given, literally, the run of the building that modern architects have made their real contributions to functional improvement in design, as in the British schools building programme that the world now recognises as one of the achievements of post-war architecture.

This habit of radical enquiry has become so engrained in the thinking of the major modern architects that they have been able to export their talents as intellectual *agents-provocateurs* into other fields—and not only of design. Most notably, Charles Eames was once retained by a major US industrial concern to interfere in its policy-making activities in other fields besides design, simply because for a man like him no routine or ritual of method and procedure is sacred or beyond investigation. Modern architects, as a profession, take it almost as a given right to apply their talents to any problem that requires solving, and as a result they have left their mark on more than just architecture. Eames, for instance, first came to world notice as the inventor of a family of metal-legged, plastic-bodied chairs that have wrought the second great revolution in furniture design in this century.

Steel and plywood chair by Charles Eames. Below: steel tube and webbing chair by Mart Stam. Facing page: steel tube and cane chair by Marcel Breuer.

The previous revolution in furniture design was also the work of architects: three of them—Mies van de Rohe, Mart Stam and Marcel Breuer—all with a pretty good claim to have invented the resilient steel-tube chair around 1927. One of their contemporaries, who hadn't invented the steel-tube chair but patently wished he had, insisted that the actual facts of authorship were unimportant compared to the 'rationalism' that had 'engendered a collective art'. Rationalism was the supposed mental discipline of the Functionalist epoch, but reason, being only a mechanical system like an electronic computer, can produce no more than has been put into it. You could feed the concepts *sit* and *tube* into a computer for a century (which was about how long massproduced metal furniture of a sort had been in existence) and nothing radical would come out. It was a series of imaginative assaults on the problem of sitting and the kind of structure that

should be associated with it, by the Dutch architect Gerrit Rietveld, without any reference to steel tube, that opened the road toward the modern metal chair.

He enquired how the body sat, and how it could be best supported in that position, and produced a wooden chair in which the surfaces on which the body rested were carefully discriminated from the structure that maintained those surfaces at the right inclination and height from the ground. The result was, in fact, more of a work of art than a fully functional machine for sitting in, but the reasonableness of the solution struck a generation of men like a shaft of light. Yet reason could not have posed the original question; only a well-trained imagination coupled with a habit of taking nothing on trust could have indicated the answer. This training, this habit of mind, are attributes that every great modern architect possesses, that every great modern school of architecture aims to inculcate in its students, and it is the impact of these twin instruments of investigation on the complex of functions old and new, that gives modern architecture its peculiar moral authority. But it hardly ever gives modern architecture its distinctive forms—even where they have acquired the vital status of the brand-image of Functionalism, their history is almost completely independent of the functions they are called upon to symbolise.

3. FORM

> ... to invent and create forms symbolising our age
> Walter Gropius

> We refuse to recognise problems of form
> Mies van der Rohe

The forms of modern architecture are a periodical embarrassment to its practitioners (the contradictory opinions, above, were uttered almost simultaneously by men employing identical architectural forms) because they are not much determined by the functions that the buildings have to perform, and not much determined by the materials of which they are constructed. Neither function nor construction is without its influence, and the man who turns with enthusiasm to new functional solutions and new structural methods is likely to turn also to new formal expressions. But to blame these innovations for the new forms of modern architecture is like blaming the saxophone for the sound of jazz, simply because it is an obvious innovation.

What is owed to functional demands is most often the general arrangement of parts—there are a strictly limited number of ways in which a flow-production factory or a main-line terminus can be laid out, and these do, indeed, tend to settle the bulk form of the total building. But not conclusively; the choice of one method of construction as against another, which may arise from quite separate considerations, will drastically affect the silhouette of that bulk against the sky, the façade it presents to the street. Ideally, form, function and construction should appear inevitable and indissoluble, and we almost expect the precise solution to be so specifically inevitable to one particular building that we may suspect it when we find it exactly repeated on another; the real criticism of plagiarism in modern architecture is not that modernists over-prize individuality, but that every building is a unique problem in its own setting and circumstances, and deserves a unique solution.

Such unique solutions are commonly feasible because modern techniques of construction make almost any form possible. A generation that has been brought up to despise the Beaux-Arts proposition '. . . . later one can show how it may be built; that is, the realisation of something already conceived', has been driven into a similar position by sheer abundance of structural ingenuity. Provided the client can foot the bill, engineers have become able to furnish architects with practically any form they want.

What forms have they wanted, and why? In the first instance they wanted clean simple forms, because all the old styles, and even Art Nouveau, had been complex and ornate. By about 1910 they were ready for someone to tell them that decoration was wrong—only to discover that the words had already been uttered, by Adolf Loos. In a brilliant, muddle-headed and highly Viennese essay entitled *Ornament and Crime*, written in 1908, he argued that ornament is not a fit occupation for a civilised man of the twentieth century, that ornament is a mark of savagery or criminal retrogression, an outlet for depraved sexuality . . . 'as a general rule, one can rank the cultures of different peoples by the extent to which their lavatory walls have been drawn upon'.

By 1914, the pioneer modernists had got the graffiti off their walls, but the walls remained surprisingly similar to most previous walls. In Germany, one Father of the Modern Movement, Peter Behrens, continued to fit industrial functions ingeniously into what were still, in total bulk, Doric temples; in France, the other Father, Auguste Perret, was using reinforced concrete to create a column and beam architecture that was entirely classical in feeling and classical also in many of its details.

This persistent classicism that the Fathers passed on to the Masters of the next generation is not to be despised; it was the unspoken code of honour that held modern architecture together in the teenage period, and underlay its choice of forms, much as the idea of the gentleman underlies the English idea of elegance.

Top: Peter Behrens, AEG turbine factory, Berlin, 1908. Bottom: Auguste Perret, Garage Ponthieu, Paris, 1906.

But while the teenage uniform was being settled, the classical prejudice operated to kill off the first crop of really original forms that the movement produced. From 1912 to 1922—from Hans Poelzig's water tower in Posen to Eric Mendelsohn's hat factory at Luckenwalde—there flourished in German-speaking countries a school of so-called expressionists who genuinely strove to find new forms for new functions. The last major work of this movement, Hugo Haering's farm at Gut Garkau, was rapidly pushed into the limbo labelled *romantic* by the uniformed conformists of the teenage period, only to emerge again with force and authority as a prophecy of what would happen to modern architecture in the nineteen-fifties: it could almost be a mature work of Alvar

Aalto, grand master of Finnish Modernism.

The way in which modern architecture has somewhat circled back on itself is an uncomfortable reminder that the supposedly rational forms of the twenties were quite as much formalist as they were functional in inspiration, and that the history of architectural form in our time has an almost independent development. Outside the classical tradition of the profession itself, those forms of the twenties had three linked sources in the traditions of modern fine art. And although those sources worked differ-

Top: water tower, Posen. Below, left to right: hat factory, Luckenwalde; farm, Gut Garkau, 1924; civic centre, Säynätsalo by Alvar Aalto, 1951.

ently on different architects, the end product was a remarkable unanimity of manner in the International Style, between 1926 and 1946.

One of these three sources has had a devious and underground effect: Futurism, with its sweeping messianic enthusiasm for 'the machine'. A literary movement in its origin, with extensive ramifications into the visual arts, it taught a generation to look for inspiration in the technology of the First Machine Age, and exalted certain forms and materials as being proper to a Machine Age art. Though spiritually bankrupt by the end of the first world war, its passing unmarked by any architectural monuments worthy of the name, its relevance to the true line of development of modern architectural form is shown in the astonishingly prophetic sketches of one of Futurism's fringe-members, Antonio Sant'Elia, which frequently anticipated the forms of the twenties.

But, more important than this, Futurism survived into the twenties as a buried moral imperative, giving power and conviction to forms drawn from the other two sources, Cubism and abstract art. From Cubism's wandering emphasis on the regular geometrical solids (canonised by Cézanne as the cylinder, sphere and cone and thus belonging to a tradition that goes back to Plato) come a group of forms, mostly cubic and rectangular, but including also cylinders and half-cylinders (handy for staircases). These forms were realised, where humanly possible, in absolute Platonic purity; cornices, cappings, sills, dripstones were rigorously suppressed, even the facts of structure were plastered over and rendered smooth to give a homogeneous surface and preserve the uninterrupted purity of the form.

This last practice, of course, makes quiet nonsense of slogans like truth to materials (the public is so confused that it believes these plastered surfaces are really reinforced concrete) and is most commonly perpetrated by Le Corbusier and the French wing of Modernism, but the most extensive justification of it,

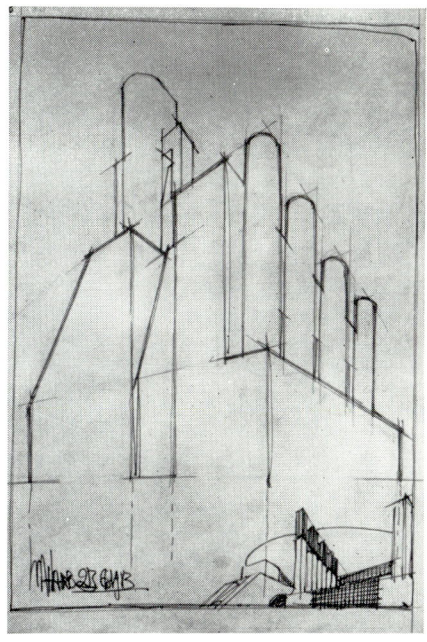

Sketch for a power station, 1913, by Sant'Elia.

on purely formalist grounds, are to be found in the writings of J. J. P. Oud, the Dutch architect who is more generally associated with the influence of abstract art on architecture. This movement, descended from both Cubism and Futurism, filled a desperate gap in the architectural thought of Holland, Germany and Russia immediately after the First World War. Form-hungry architects fastened on the work of Malevitsch, Lissitsky, Mondriaan and van Doesburg, and extracted from it a repertoire of rectangular forms and a set of rules of protocol for introducing them to one another. In this they were energetically assisted by the artists themselves, who believed that their art had immediate architectural relevance. Both Lissitsky and van Doesburg were active propagandists, and the latter ran a magazine under the title of *de Stijl*, that helped to make the abstract art movement aware of itself at an international level.

Nevertheless, that internationalism ran only on a line from Amsterdam to Moscow at first and left France untouched. Le Corbusier's work—say, the villa Cook—in 1926 is not very like one of Mies van der Rohe's works of the same period, such as his monument to the Communist martyrs Karl Liebknecht and Rosa Luxemburg. Yet a year later the French and German schools, Cubist and abstract, had fused into a single style. For

J. J. P. Oud, born in 1890, is conspicuous in the twenties; he was the first to reveal, in any substantial body of work, the temper, preoccupations and preferred architectural forms of the budding International Style. With van Doesburg he was one of the founders of the *Stijl* group in 1917, but its aesthetic extremism soon repelled his craftsmanly mind, and he was one of the first to resign.

a stirring moment at the Weissenhof exhibition of 1927, they stood before the world united in forms and intentions; the show houses designed by Gropius, Oud, Mies, Le Corbusier and others were so much of one mind that Alfred H. Barr coined the term *International Style* to describe it.

Poised for world conquest, the new architecture discovered that it had a uniform by which friend could be distinguished from foe, a uniform whose adoption indicated that its wearer wanted to be considered as one of the gang. For twenty years—thirty in the case of some critics—the defence of modern architecture was the defence of that uniform quite as much as the defence of Functionalism, and there are many people today who cannot accept a building as functional unless it wears the uniform rig.

But already in the early thirties, Le Corbusier was adjusting his dress, and incorporating sporting or tweedy elements not accepted by the rest of the gang. At Mathes, on the Biscay coast, he built a little holiday house with pitched roofs and random masonry walls and rough carpenter's woodwork. Romantic, the critics decided between alarm and admiration, while Le Corbu-

Facing page, top: Villa Cook. Bottom left: Liebknecht-Luxemburg monument; right: Weissenhof exhibition. This page: house at Mathes.

sier himself went off to South America, there to inspire in Brazil a group of young (or youngish) architects to create the first *national* style of modern architecture. From Lucio Costa's Ministry of Education in Rio, obviously Corb-inspired, to Oscar Niemeyer's government buildings in the all-new capital city of Brasilia, this style has been the envy of the world—and played havoc with the forms of the teenage uniform. It has kept the tall slab shapes, often raised on stilts in the Corbusian manner, it has kept the smooth surfaces—sometimes—and the simple geometry —when it feels like it—but it has carried them all to a degree of freedom so marked and so personal that the Italian critic Gillo Dorfles has, with some justification, termed it Neo-Baroque.

All this was implicit in Le Corbusier's own style, anyhow, as his recent work in India will testify. All that has happened to modern architecture since the International Style broke up is that different schools and different individuals have pursued aspects and possibilities of the style to their logical-illogical conclusions. The Brazilians went one way; Mies van der Rohe and his followers went another, driving the narrow logic of frame construction to a condition where his followers have given US big business a uniform as correct, well-cut and standardised as a Brooks Brothers suit. Others again, stimulated by the emergence of great engineers like Pierluigi Nervi or Felix Candela have brought the Modern Movement's long-ingrained admiration of engineers out into the open as frank imitation of their forms: sincere flattery indeed, though often with insufficient knowledge of constructional maths to ensure that these forms can be built as they have been designed.

In all these developments one thing is certain: that they are outgrowths of the International Style. Sensing an excess of refinement, some young and not-so-young architects have tried to back out of this formal free-for-all, and recapture virtues they feel to be mislaid today. Some merely revive the shapes and details of primitive Modernism—the Neoliberty movement, or

Art Nouveau revival in Italy is an example—and some try to recover the heroic stance and dogmatic certainty of an earlier day—the New Brutalists in England.

Out of all this there emerges a situation where an irregular, almost windowless brick box, a lattice dome covered with transparent plastic, or a square tower of tinted glass, will all be recognised as modern *by their forms*—pretty much as the family likeness of French, Norwegian and Greek will be recognised by a student of languages. What these various manifestations of modern have in common is not easy to put into words, though a smattering acquaintance with modern architecture will soon begin to suggest affinities to an observant eye. Their minimum common property is that they are not like any forms in the architecture that was before 1900. Their first positive property in common is that they all have parallels, however devious, with the other plastic arts of their common period. The next is that they take extreme advantage of new constructional materials, and new constructional techniques; in the extended sense that where brickwork appears in an unmistakably modern context, it is not walling built according to the rule of the bricklayer's practised thumb, but apt to be calculated brickwork, treated by the same kind of slide-rule disciplines as prestressed concrete or extruded aluminium. If new materials have not been altogether decisive in determining the forms of modern architecture, new ways of thinking about structure lie very close in places, and it is now time to examine the relationship of thought and material in modern construction.

Facing page, top: Ministry of Education, Rio de Janeiro; Middle: parliament buildings, Brasilia; bottom: exhibition hall, Turin, by Pier Luigi Nervi. This page: Pepsi-Cola building, New York, by Gordon Bunshaft of Skidmore, Owings and Merrill.

4. CONSTRUCTION

> ... with raw materials to construct moving relationships
> Le Corbusier

In Paris in the early twenties it was possible to talk as if modern architecture had been caused by reinforced concrete. Certainly there was some exciting concrete-work to be seen, but Auguste Perret's concrete church of Notre Dame du Raincy was hardly modern, and Freyssinet's heroic hangars at Orly were hardly architecture. As far as buildings that could be called modern architecture were concerned, there was no concrete to be seen at all: surfaces were neatly rendered and painted over to conceal the fact that concrete often had to share the structure with cinder blocks, pot tiles or even—save the mark!—bricks. The budgets on which pioneer modern buildings were constructed were commonly too tight to admit of any larking about with untried materials or experimental constructional techniques, and even where finance permitted them, local building regulations usually didn't. Modernity lay in the functional planning, the forms of the exterior, and was spread thinly over the surfaces to conceal the unmodern materials of which the structure was built.

Why this sensitivity about materials, the desire to make the

Left: Church of Notre Dame du Raincy. Right: Airship hangar at Orly.

house look modern-built? In Holland, W. M. Dudok successfully combined the forms of modernity with brick surfaces; the result was a rave success in middle-of-the-road countries like England, but universally execrated among convinced modernists, clearly because they felt that brick was in itself a betrayal of the aims of the modern movement. It was, of course, an offence against the clean-wall orthodoxy deriving from Adolf Loos's bent puritanism, but it was rarely combated on those terms—it was the idea of a solid load-bearing wall that was abhorrent, and it was always construction, not aesthetics, that formed the hub of controversy.

The reasons were complex. One of them is embedded deep in the history of the idea of modern architecture. Early in the new century, Hermann Muthesius drew attention to the splendours of the constructional masterpieces of Victorian engineering, such as the Crystal Palace and the Eiffel tower, and bade his followers pay attention to them. Twenty-five years later, Sigfried Giedion's book *Bauen im Frankreich* resumed the theme and extended it to cover more recent work in reinforced concrete as well as the earlier work in iron. But he also drew direct parallels between the early masterpieces of engineering and the work being done by his own friends and contemporaries, implying some similarity of method or intention. This was gratifying, because it gave the new-fledged International Style a reputable ancestry; but how real was it?

Psychologically, it was real enough—the whole generation was abnormally sensitive to the aesthetics of engineering work, and most held the *Grands Constructeurs* of the previous century in genuine esteem. Furthermore, they were attached emotionally to engineering materials by a tradition extending from the Futurists, who had praised steel, concrete, glass, plastics, lightweight and impermanent materials, and damned bronze, marble and other monumental stuff; Le Corbusier spoke in this tradition when he praised aircraft as 'little houses that fly and yet can

Willem Marinus Dudok, born 1884, represents a strain of Dutch architecture slightly more traditionalist than Oud's; hence his sprint from thatched romanticism to square brick modern was the more spectacular. Hilversum Town Hall, above, his masterpiece, will stand re-examination; the rest has been lost in the dust as the rest of the Modern Movement went galloping past and left him far behind.

resist tempests'. Associated with the tradition at this point is the mystique of prefabrication that gripped most of the masters of that time, the mass-produced house made in a factory out of lightweight modern materials. Some of the prestige of such a structure was felt to rub off on other structures built, or even appearing to be built out of the same materials.

Behind this again lurks the mystique of the engineer as the noble savage of the machine age: a mystique owed partly to Adolf Loos (like so many radical myths of our time) who always admired what he believed to be unselfconsciousness in design, and partly to the Futurist Marinetti (like so many more of our myths) who professed to see in engineers the outlines of an alien culture 'the gift of mechanical prophecy, the flair for metals'. By the early twenties, Le Corbusier was giving engineers the full noble savage treatment 'healthy and virile, active and useful, balanced and happy in their work'. Modified over the years, some version of this proposition has always persisted since, and even when architects fear and envy engineers who threaten to take away their work, they are still prepared to admire to distraction any engineer whose work seems moderately sympathetic to them.

Le Corbusier's circle admired Freyssinet, without showing the slightest desire to employ his forms or his methods; the contemporary *G*-group in Berlin admired Matte-Trucco's super-Futurist car-factory at Turin with a race-track on its roof. The followers of Siegfried Giedion in the thirties admired the bridges of the Swiss engineer Robert Maillart, while the first generation of outright modernists in Britain could find no praise too high for the work of the engineer Owen Williams. After the war, a growing wave of admiration for the vaultwork of Pierluigi Nervi was the prelude to a cult of engineers such as modern architecture had not seen before, and the cult did not lack cult-objects and heroes—after Nervi came Torroja, Catalano, Candela, Buckminster Fuller, Defaille, Frei Otto and a host of others.

Left: Schwandbach bridge by Maillart.
Right: Fiat factory, Turin.

But this time, the part played by the engineers in determining architectural form was real. Influential sections of the Modern Movement around 1950 were in the mood for a revolt against the rectangular rectitude of the teenage uniform; the emergence of a new generation (*sic*: Fuller was in his fifties) advocating a new principle of construction (*sic* again: the vault, almost as old as architecture) was the vital coincidence and the Modern Movement has been in uproar ever since. But there really was something new in this situation, however—the application of new techniques of thought to curved structures had at last made a mass breakthrough.

In earlier days, Freyssinet, Maillart, Nervi, had made only tentative and marginal assaults on the problem of vaulting, but they and their contemporaries had begun to accumulate a body of experience, to which the application of radical methods of tensioning the reinforcement in concrete shells, and the application of radical geometrical techniques in built-up structures, came as the last liberating gesture. There followed a revolution that appears to be more profound than that brought on by the first discovery of reinforced concrete or framed construction.

The freedoms originally brought to architecture by reinforced concrete and metal framing had less to do with the ability to project cantilevers etc., than with reducing the mass of supporting structure at ground level. Columns could be slighter and further apart, thick supporting walls were no longer necessary. These

Freyssinet, Hennebique and the rest of the pioneers of reinforced concrete are admirably chronicled in the early part of Peter Collins's valuable, if idiosyncratic, study *Concrete, the Vision of a New Architecture*.

advantages were not essential to the creation of large buildings serving modern functions—as witness the tall Monadnock office block in Chicago, entirely in load-bearing masonry. Nor did architects at once scramble to secure the advantages that framed structure could offer, not until a variety of other influences had altered their aesthetic outlook. The house that François Hennebique built for himself in 1904 as a demonstration of the potentialities of concrete looks humorous rather than prophetic because its style is so gauche and disorganised, whereas Auguste Perret's block in the rue Franklin looks far more convincing, in spite of its less adventurous construction, because it has about it a whiff of the new aesthetic and a genuinely radical plan; required by town-planning laws to make a light well through the block, Perret put it on the front instead of the back, giving all rooms views across the Seine, instead of making half of them look into a cramped couryard.

In other words, when a new kind of form and a new kind of plan were wanted, the constructional means were there to achieve them, the means being the steel or concrete frame, with its narrow supports and wide spans, its ability to stand narrow on the ground, straddle roads, send out cantilevers and accept any sort of skin from solid stone to transparent glass or even nothing at all—at the top of Perret's block the frame suddenly erupts, free and unencumbered, into two little loggie.

The second structural revolution was of the same order, only more so. Vaulting suddenly became easy—there is no other way to express it. The last great vault of the experimental period had been Max Berg's superlative *Jahrhunderthalle* of 1913 in Breslau, massive, monumental, profoundly exciting but far too solid in its members to look easy. The vault that opened the second revolution was not massive, nor monumental. Felix Candela's Cosmic Ray Pavilion for the University of Mexico is no bigger than most houses, and its smallness was part of the attraction. It could be visualised as part of a larger structure, the quantities

Top: Monadnock office block. Below: Hennebique's house. Facing page, left to right, top: flats in the rue Franklin, Paris; *Jahrhunderthalle*; Cosmic Ray Pavilion. Below: inside and outside of cardboard dome Milan, 1954.

of materials and labour were such as could be encompassed in a passing thought—a few builders trowelling on a couple of truckloads of cement by hand—the formwork was ordinary old planks of wood, and the designer was reputed to have done the maths in his head.

At about the same time, the ability of other simple materials to produce sophisticated structures was being demonstrated in Milan, where, at the Tenth Triennale, there were shown two of Buckminster Fuller's domes made of sheets of cardboard cut and scored, for all the world like making up the models on the back of cereal packets, joined together with something for all the world like an ordinary office stapler, and covered by a membrane for all the world like a domestic polythene bag. Yet it is Candela's shuttering that really marks the epoch, because it had always been the argument from shuttering that was the last ditch defence of the rectangular framed structure which—literally—supported the rectangular uniform of teenage modern. Because concrete had to be poured in wooden moulds, which were cheapest to make from straight planks, concrete would be square, even if it performed better in multi-curved vaults, because curved shuttering was ruinously expensive to set up. But now Candela showed that by picking the right geometric form—such as a hyperboloid, called a 'ruled form' because it was generated by straight lines—you could get complex three-dimensional curves out of simple plank shuttering. So far this dramatic extension of the powers of the plain piece of wood applies only via the hyperboloid family: the warped slab, the hyperboloid of rotation and the hyperbolic paraboloid, but there are so many of them that their end is nowhere near in sight yet. In addition, they are mostly structurally sound: that familar hyperboloid of rotation, the cooling tower, is a case in point, so that they cannot be brushed off as mere formalist whimsy.

Be it also noted, that these unexplored extensions of structural possibility have been caused by thinking, not new materials. The amount of life in the old materials is extraordinary: concrete is fighting back with all sorts of new pre- and post-tensioning systems, as well as in lightweight forms; wood in laminates, boards, and built-up beams, as well as in panels where it is associated with metals and plastics; a new method of structural analysis—the plastic theory—has given new life to steel framing. All this before we even begin to consider plastics as such. This class of materials, however, still seems to be languishing in the condition of concrete before Auguste Perret: it is looking for a master who will give it form, and the only real candidate so far is Ionel Schein, the newest hero of the mass-production dream. It has been suggested that the forms of plastics are being invented elsewhere in another material—by Le Corbusier's recent work in concrete—and if that is so, the old rationalist dogma about technique dictating form will have to be pensioned off for good. It has done the Modern Movement good service as a creative myth, but new materials no longer serve to explain what is new about modern architecture. Neither brick nor fibreglass account for the modern architect's radical attitude to function, nor do they inhibit him in applying it; neither steel nor concrete account for, and neither is necessary to, the modern architect's radical conception of space.

Plastic motel unit by Ionel Schein.

5. SPACE

> The experience of space is not a privilege of the gifted few, but a biological function.
> Moholy-Nagy

The one thing that is undeniably new about modern architecture is the conscious manipulation of space. We talk loosely about Baroque space and Gothic space and argue about whether the Greeks ever had any sense of space at all; but the ability even to utter the phrase 'architectural space' is an achievement of the late nineteenth century, and a critic's term, or an historian's in the first place. For an architect to think of himself as using or working in space is purely twentieth-century, and one of the things that marks the modern architect over and above any considerations of formal style. But, in addition to this primary cast of mind, the space in which the modern architect consciously works is unlike the space, conscious or otherwise, of any previous architecture.

For most of history, space has existed only inside structures—outside was only nature, chaos, the unmeasurable. Nothing shows this better than the dull exteriors and splendid interiors of Roman baths, or the way that Gothic masons drove stone structure to its logical and unreasonable conclusions in order to create interiors of tremendous height and grace—all that fretwork on the outside was just scaffolding. Renaissance men reversed the process, and could see the outsides of their buildings—as the Greeks did—as isolated works of art. Unlike the Greeks they contrived small, boxy, perspective-centred spaces around them, but those spaces were interiors, closed in by the façades that flanked the piazza, spaces furnished by the buildings they contained.

Baroque space admitted of infinity—perhaps, but we must be wary of reading Baroque mathematics into Baroque planning without good warrant. But this infinity was more usually symbolised than admitted: symbolised by the obelisk that focused the vista, the light falling on the altar at the end of a dark nave. And this was infinity counted from zero at an observer standing in the right place—once you stray from the portico that commands the avenue, the entrance on the axis of the church, any possible relationship with infinity evaporates.

In the nineteenth century, Baroque planning concepts were stretched to breaking; with the aid of a railway ticket you could travel in a day far beyond the limits of any conceivable architectural composition, and spatial infinity began to be detached from any conceivable view or vista. Physical distance shrank decade by decade, and when a real man could wager to circle the globe in eighty days the roundness of the world became more nearly tangible than when Puck offered to girdle it in forty minutes. When Lindberg flew on schedule from New York to Paris, continental togetherness had arrived, and the world became, in Buckminster Fuller's radical intuition, a single landmass at the bottom of an ocean of air.

Bottle Evolving in Space by Boccioni. Below: Picasso's *Girl with the Mandoline*.

Infinity had begun to enter the consciousness of plastic artists a little before this, around the time that avant-gardists of all sorts began to acquire the habit of talking of space-time and the fourth dimension. By 1911-12, the Cubist painters of Paris, casually dropping fragments of Einsteinian jargon, were painting pictures whose space, though far from infinite, was not focussed on the perspective conventions of a fixed vanishing point and an ideal viewing point. A picture like Picasso's *Girl with the Mandoline*, has no vanishing point and its shallow space is equally convincing from any viewpoint, near or far, so long as it is somewhere in front of the picture. About the same time, the Italian Futurists, twitting the Cubists for slack terminology, were thinking of space as being focussed by the objects in it, almost irrespective of any observer. For them, space was the interpenetrating spheres of influence of adjacent objects. Somewhere between these two concepts, of an even and unfocussed space, however limited, and an infinite space defined by the matter in it, the basic space concept of modern architecture appeared, first formulated by Dutch and Russian abstract artists, but built by Frenchmen like Le Corbusier quite as much as any Germans.

In this concept, space is firstly infinite, and extends unrestrainedly in all directions (though it is not, in practice, handled as if its upward and downward extensions were of great interest). Secondly, this space is measured, defined, made apprehensible by some sort of invisible structure or geometry. Usually, this mental structure is rectangular, and architecture is conceived almost as a kind of three-dimensional cross-word, with some squares filled in, some left blank, some of the lines between them thickened up. In some of Le Corbusier's most sophisticated works, like the Villa Savoie, the structure keeps bursting into view, in the form of columns rising awkwardly in the middle of the room, or just clear of the wall (the same thing also happens in Mies van der Rohe's work around 1930). These columns are part of the regular structural frame, they represent the geometric order of space; the walls are inserted *ad hoc*, they represent the architect's free play with and upon that space.

Rectangularity, though, is not a pre-requisite. When entering one of Buckminster Fuller's domes for the first time, one receives a most emphatic sensation of space, modern space, if not square space. But all his domes do possess a very regular and emphatic structure, which gives a powerful sense of being caged in a pervasive geometry, and they often have a translucent covering which admits light, and thus implies space, evenly from all directions.

But, thirdly, the space of modern architecture is conceived as having a very special relationship to the observer: either he, or it, is in motion (in an age that thinks much about relativity, it doesn't much matter which moves). This concept is more allegorical than physical, but its psychological reality is vital to modern architecture. In one way, the interior spaces of a building are to be experienced as a series of partitions of infinite space by an observer moving through them on a prescribed route—*route* is the very word used by Le Corbusier in connection with the ramps of the Villa Savoie—indicated by stairs, platforms, ramps, even the pattern or texture of the floor, which guide him through a series of spatial manoeuvres. Perhaps the best example of this in England is provided by the foyers of the Festival Hall; in America, by the ramps of the Guggenheim Museum.

Immediately below: foyers of the Festival Hall. Bottom: the Guggenheim Museum, by Frank Lloyd Wright. The central space is surrounded by a continuously climbing spiral ramp.

The opposite case of space moving from, or round, a still observer is not altogether removed from the preceding one in physical fact, but its metaphysical content is more subtle. It has been with us as a working concept ever since the masters of the twenties introduced the idea of the interpenetration of inner and outer space, house and garden. Space in this sense flows almost tidally, away from the observer—when he is outside the house, space flows in, when he is within, space flows out into the garden. That space flows away from the observer can be taken as axiomatic: he is the source of spatial experience. It is also pretty well axiomatic that it flows along a discernible route, and flows out of sight. Space, in modern architecture, does not flow from the centre of a simple square room—there one experiences only a still, 'Renaissance' space. It flows round corners, over the edges of balconies, along corridors, up some staircases but not all, and round and behind obstacles and free-standing objects of all kinds.

The epitome of all this kind of spatiality is probably Mies van de Rohe's Farnsworth House, outside Chicago. Space exists there between two given planes, the floor slab and the roof slab, and has no upward or downward extensions whatsoever, except that some sensitive spirits feel that it flows down the four little steps from the floor slab to the terrace. These two limiting slabs are also the only opaque surfaces on the exterior of the house,

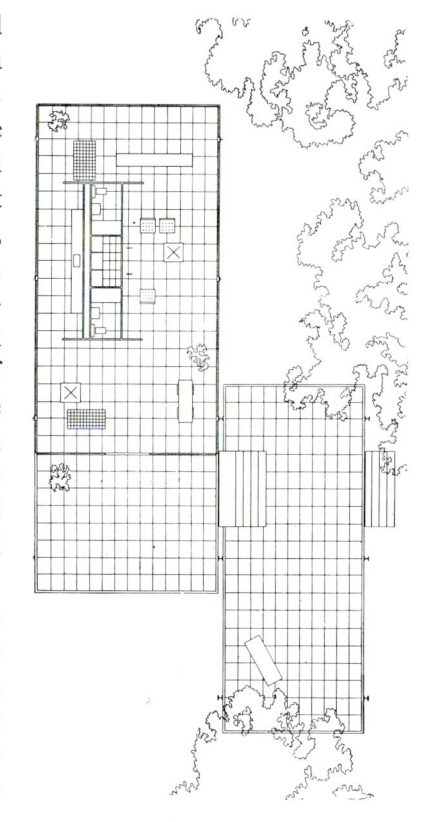

Farnsworth House, Fox River, Illinois; plan above.

everything else is floor to ceiling glass, or nothing at all. As a result the interior space is in almost total communication with the infinite space outside, visually speaking—so much in communication with infinity that some visitors feel a sense of risk from stepping off the edge of the floor-slab. Between the upper and lower slab there are no visible connections, except the six regularly spaced uprights of the structure which contain an implication of extending beyond the roof slab, so that—allegorically speaking, and viewed from outside—there are some hints of vertical extension into infinity. But only hints: the dominant visual function of those verticals is to establish the regular rhythm that measures, controls, the piece of infinite space that has been marked off to form the house. The only other vertical member that reaches from floor to ceiling is a free-standing construction that functions as a fireplace on one side, and as a kitchen unit on the other, and this is an almost text-book example of the kind of object around which space most persuasively flows, an effect that is amply aided—as in many of Mies's works—by the evident continuity of the floor surface.

This may be the epitome, and a small masterpiece of modern space, but it is not a *great* masterpiece of modern space. The two great masterpieces both antedate the modern movement completely. One was the old Crystal Palace, built out of repetitive glass and iron units for the Great Exhibition of 1851. It was archaic, primitive, but it was so big that it seemed to contain

Interiors of Farnsworth House.

Below: the Crystal Palace as re-erected at Sydenham.

infinity within itself, the space running off endlessly as far as the eye could see, measured off by the regular module of the structure till it flickered away in an optical haze compounded of distance and light. If that was archaic, the mature masterpiece of modern space, vast, overwhelming, mocking everything that has been put up since, is the Eiffel Tower. Here, every variety of modern spatial experience, plus some that are unique to the Tower, is piled on the viewer in such abundance that he begins to feel insecure and disoriented. Here is participation in infinity, the more convincing because of the great heights involved; here is space that flows away behind structure and spills down stairways; here is space through which the observer moves, either under his own power, or by a variety of different sorts of lifts.

But underlying all, and more fantastic than all, is the structure of the Tower itself, the geometry that controls all spaces. No simple system of regular horizontals and verticals, this great space frame, constructed to battle the wind rather than gravity (Eiffel was one of the pioneers of wind-tunnel testing) occasionally supports a horizontal surface—as a concession to human weakness, one feels—but is, in itself, a system of interlacing diagonals bracing main members that sag not towards the earth's centre, but towards the horizon. Nothing else on earth gives so powerful a sensation of being in free space, free of any reference to the gravity-dominated structures of all other architectural space. Even on the substantial staircases that thread through the lower legs of the structure, an observer feels no sure faith that gravity will go on acting in the same direction after he has turned the next landing; space seems to extend in all directions, globally, indiscriminately around him. It will probably all seem very dull and old hat to men who have actually experienced free fall in outer space, but, as we stand, this old masterpiece offers the earth-bound tourist the surest preview he can have of the spatial experiences of his descendants.

To stand on this seventy-year-old staircase, and experience

The Eiffel Tower. Bottom: upward view.

this free crazy space, is to know something essential about modern architecture. It has grown up, thrown off its teenage uniform, but it still has not equalled the achievement of this pioneer space-machine that is older than all but a handful of the architects practising today. Modern architecture, then, has not yet drawn all the dividends on the capital of spatial, structural, formal and functional concepts that were invested for it before birth, let alone the compound interest of new ideas and new techniques that has accrued to it since. Architecture, now, given the self-confidence and sense of purpose acquired in the disciplined, dogmatic decades of the teenage years, is just beginning to measure and assess the true possibilities that open before it. Development will be dynamic, and much that has only just become familiar will disappear.

Forms will go first, have gone already; the children of fashion and the other arts, they are expendable. Structural systems will go down too, but not so fast. They will go down in their time like forest giants whose root strength has been sapped by newer growths. But there will be new growth; new materials and techniques appear by the week. Those who have believed that modernity resided in certain forms and certain structures, will see *their* modern architecture fading before their eyes. The concept of modern architecture as a glazed cube, in Robin Boyd's phrase, is now no more, still quoting Robin Boyd, than a functional neurosis.

Those who see the physical part of modern architecture as the radical solution of functional problems, indissolubly wedded to an aesthetic part that is the manipulation of an infinite, measured and mobile space, will not be disappointed: except by the fashiony pseudo-modern that second-rate architects will put up for fashiony weak-kneed clients. But the man who checks for function and space will know true modern when he sees it, and will know that because it is true it is good—as with any other architecture the world has known.

Another view, further up the Eiffel Tower.

The Zaanstraat block: post office end, at the apex of the triangle.

Flats on the Zaanstraat, Amsterdam
Michel de Klerk

Michel de Klerk has nothing to do with the characteristic architectural developments of our century, except that he worked in it, was inspired by at least two of the architects (Berlage and Wright) who inspired many highly characteristic twentieth-century architects, and—like those architects—he worked in the field of public housing and on the scale of the modern city. In spite of an early death in 1923, he never became a posthumous legend, and, until quite recently his name and reputation were kept alive only by odd-balls like Bruno Taut.

Yet, to encounter his masterpiece, the great triangular block of flats in the angle of the Zaanstraat in Amsterdam, is to be whacked on the head by one of the most violent architectural experiences this century has produced. It is truly an '*architecture autre*', the missing complement of the modern architecture that in fact happened, but might have turned out like this, instead, but for one or two minute shifts of opinion in Europe around 1910. The assurance with which de Klerk encompasses the changing functions and considerable size of this large island site (of which only one small part is not from his designs) bespeaks a born architect and a master organiser. The management of the western end, the base of the triangle, baroque in concept but sharpened with an art-nouveau wit, is almost inconceivable in the same generation as J. J. P. Oud, with his straight rows of primly square buildings; except that Amsterdam was, for about five years, full of architects who, under de Klerk's leadership, differed from him only in not possessing his touch of genius. His chosen materials were brick, wood, tile-hanging —everything that Oud professed to hate—handled with a loving, craftsmanly care that de Klerk, quite as much as Oud, derived from Berlage. The more alien de Klerk looks to the Modern Movement, the closer he, in fact, stands to it: the long 'zeppelin' windows near the point are entirely post-futurist with a touch of Frank Lloyd Wright, and the post office with its round tower that occupies the point of the triangle is, *mutatis mutandis*, the right-handed brother of the left-handed façade of Mendelsohn's Schocken store in Stuttgart.

Just behind the post office, inside the block, is a little triangular courtyard from which one looks down the gardens in the middle of the island towards a cottage building that serves as a sort of

Michel de Klerk, 1884-1923, was the last of the romantic, short-lived prodigy pioneers, an immensely inventive but literally sick talent. He and his Amsterdam contemporaries, like Piet Kramer, pushed the structural implications of Art Nouveau beyond even the point where they had been abandoned by Mackintosh.

Facing page: above: the base of the triangle. Below: interior court with common-room building.

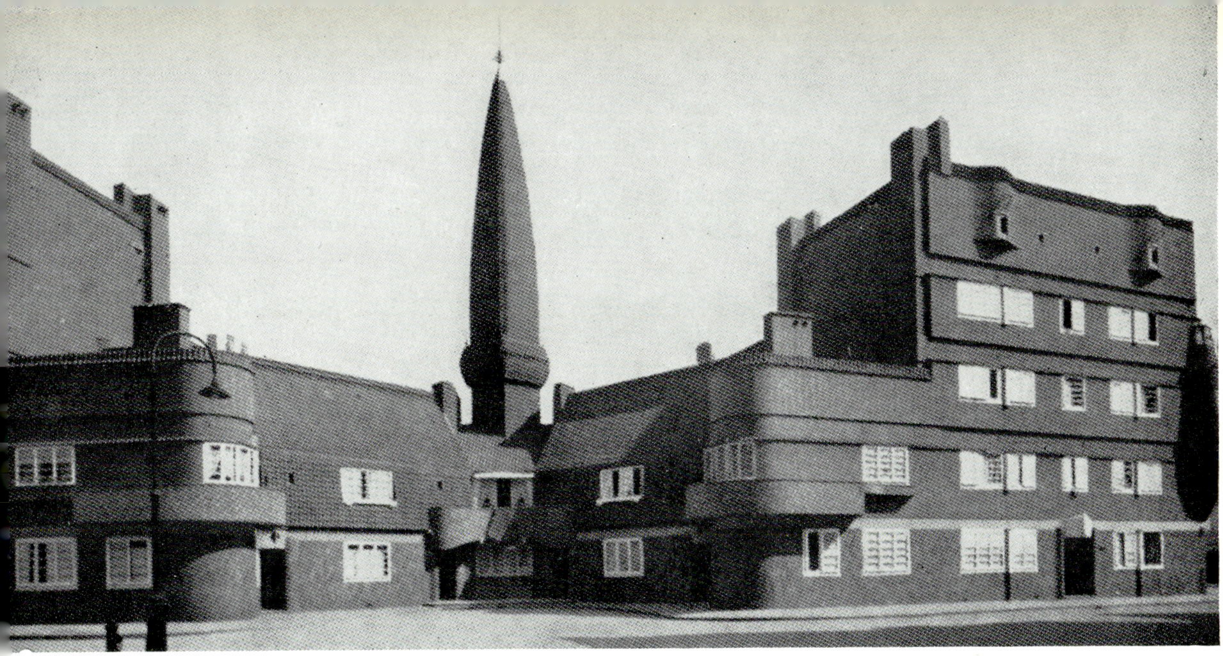

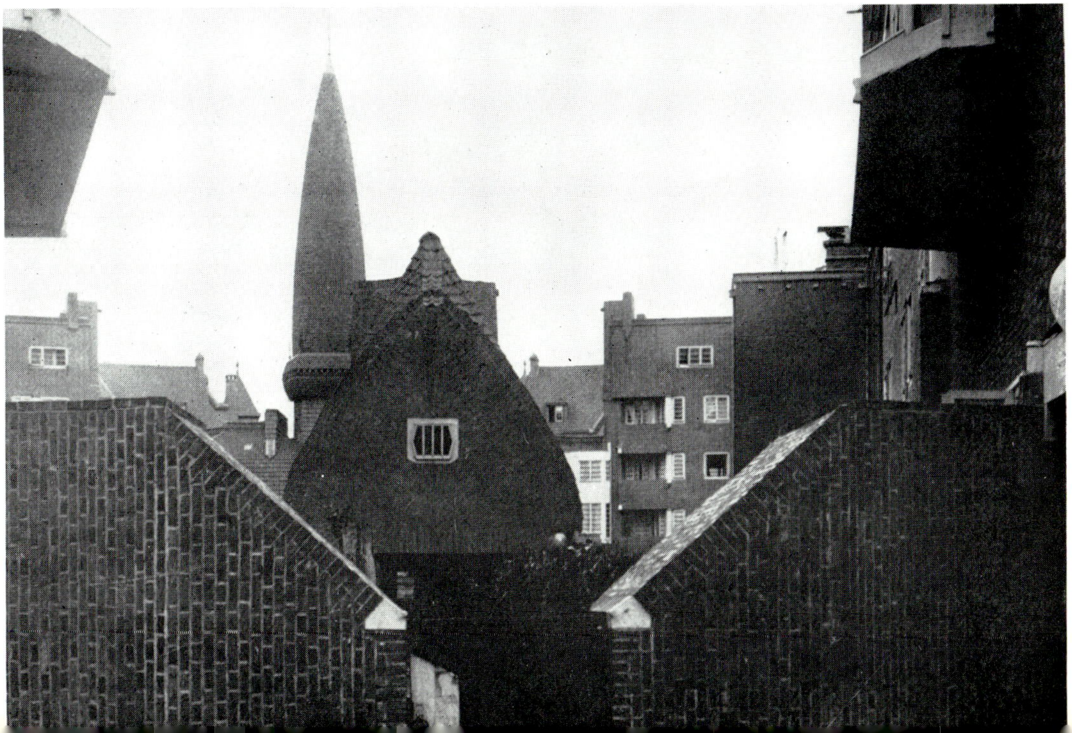

tenants' common room. The space of this little court is invaded by balconies, steps, porches, oriels, lamps, beams and other structural-functional elements, that carve in from all sides until one begins to feel a bit like the lady in the box through which the magician sticks swords and spears. This is space architecture as surely as anything spare, rectangular and undecorated, produced by the Bauhaus or the Russian Constructivists. This has the mood of the age, a little prematurely perhaps (but what about Mackintosh?) in everything, except that it is decorated. This is what modern architecture was going to look like until Adolf Loos, with his anathema on decoration, and the abstractionists, with their alternative vocabulary of undecorated forms, gave it two minute deflections from its original orbit, and ultimately set it rotating about other suns. Viewing the Zaanstraat with eyes from which all prejudice has been shocked away, one realises what a near thing it must have been.

The Schröder House, Utrecht
Gerrit T. Rietveld

A cardboard Mondriaan: so it was once called, more in perplexity than derision. It is one of two works of world consequence by Rietveld—the other is his famous 'red-blue' chair—and yet, when one looks at it, there could hardly be a less likely candidate for fame. Tiny, structurally timid, badly sited, undistinguished in plan, it may once have had compelling local and private virtues for its inhabitants that are now difficult to make convincing to outsiders, but what assures it its place in the world scene is its exterior. Here for the first time, in 1924, the aesthetic possibilities of the hard school of modern architecture were uncomprisingly and brilliantly revealed (no early house of Le Corbusier is comparable until 1926, his first vintage year). The small cube of the house expands in a proliferation of flyaway

G. T. Rietveld, born in 1888, has been mentioned already for his other significant contribution to modern design, the 'red/blue' chair (p. 29). No-one, not even his official biographer, Theodore M. Brown, has yet been able to suggest why this very competent, but otherwise unremarkable provincial figure should *twice* have contributed such symptomatic objects to the rise of the Modern Movement.

Schröder House.

planes, horizontal and vertical, that sometimes collide in right-angled intersections. There may be a long-range debt to Wright, but the implications of Wright's domestic space-games have been purged and made clean through the aesthetic detergency of European abstract art. The surfaces are, indeed, as smooth and as neutral as those of a Mondriaan painting, and in similar colours, relieved only by a use of glass that emphasises its immaterial quality (unlike the jewelled presence of the glass in Wright's Robie House) and by a few lean, sparse metal stanchions that support the edges of some of the flying planes, and steam-pipe hand-rails that make some of the planes usable as balconies. Machine aesthetic; rectangular space play: the bare minimum of the modern architecture that was to be.

Flats in St James's Place, London
Denys Lasdun

A luxury building is still not an easy assignment for an English architect to undertake (maybe this is an aspect of the conscience of the architectural profession that should be nurtured for the common good) since modern architecture here has grown up so closely with progressive politics that non-proletarian housing is still something of a moral embarrassment to us. It's easier, in some ways, for us to build, and criticise, Stirling and Gowan's picturesque, atmospheric and studiedly graceless exercise in working-class re-housing at Preston, than Eric Lyons's relaxed, eye-soothing—but middle-class—housing for the various S P A N developments around London. But it may be that the middle is the real problem, not the ends of the social spectrum, for Denys Lasdun has worked with complete conviction at both extremes: his cluster-block slum-clearance housing in Bethnal Green, and his almost overpoweringly luxurious block of skip-level flats down a turning off St James's, overlooking Green Park.

Opposite top: St James's Place flats from Green Park. Below, left to right: housing at Preston; SPAN housing at Ham Common; Bethnal Green cluster block.

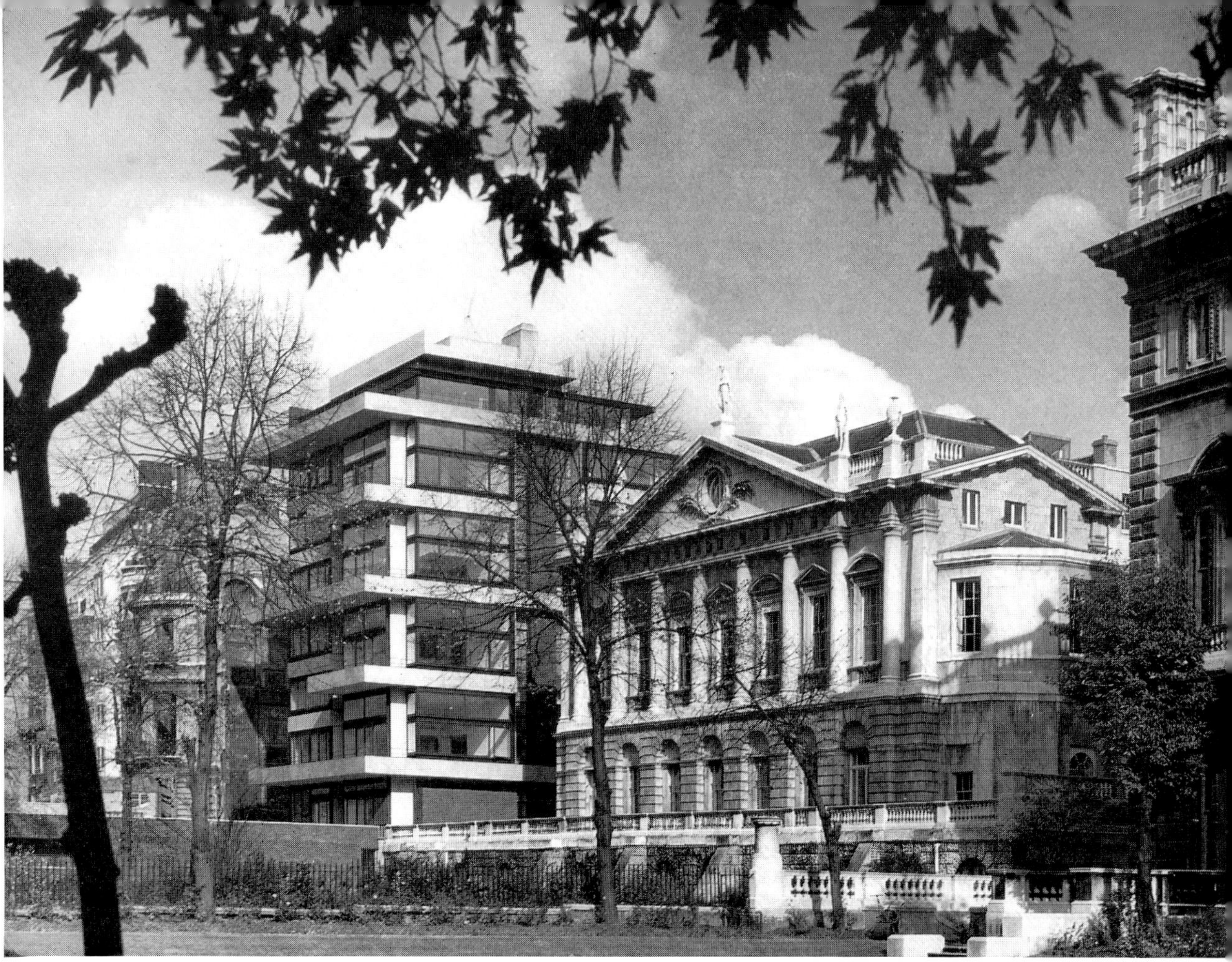

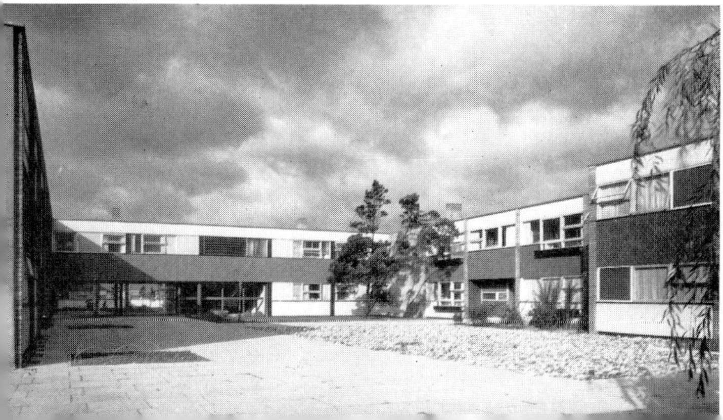

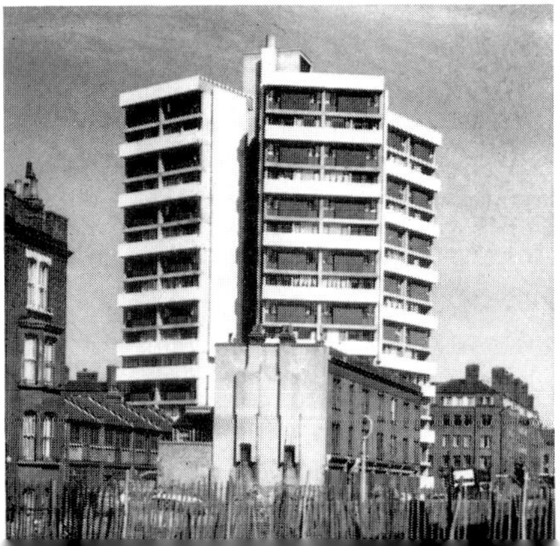

Lasdun's success in St James is basically that he has created luxury in terms of unmistakably modern architecture, and by the architectural means that are peculiar to the Modern Movement. Not fringed drapes and ankle-deep carpets but the basic luxuries of expansive spaces and lavish mechanical services. By post-war British standards the spaces are enormous, and in the one-and-a-half storey living rooms one swims, adrift in sheer volume. On the services side, the heating is conspicuously adequate, the kitchens mechanised to the eyebrows and, above all, the sound insulation is of TV-studio quality. It is London's most comprehensive demonstration of what modern architecture has to offer in the sense of a controlled and euphoric environment, physically and aesthetically satisfying before any stick of furniture or work of art has been installed.

Best of all, Lasdun has made the emphasis on space and services the source of expression on the exterior. The skip-level section, with its one-and-a-half storey units introducing a contrapuntal rhythm in the stacking of the floors, gives him almost sufficient subtleties of proportion and pattern to be able to do without any further architecture on the exterior: all that is to be seen are the edges of the balconies (which become the spandrels where the windows are up flush with the façade) establishing the main horizontals, and the ducts for the services, establishing the main verticals. Such extravagant simplicity needs to be almost offensively well detailed—and is. The vertical ducts are built of a rich dark brick as used in engineering, and the balcony fronts have aprons of choice marbles (pieces were sent back, if not choice enough). The windows are carried in bronze frames of conspicuously *de luxe* specification, and the exposed concrete work of the pent-house structure has been so skilfully poured, into shuttering so carefully built, out of what appears to be planks specially selected for their grain patterns, that shaggy old Brutalist shutter-patterned concrete is transmuted into an exquisite fine-art material.

Denys Lasdun, born 1914, is one of the most striking figures to emerge in British architecture in the fifties. Once regarded as something of a formalist (on the strength of works such as the Hallfield housing in Paddington, which he did in collaboration with Tecton) he is now held in high esteem in the profession for his insistence on basic social, human and architectural values.

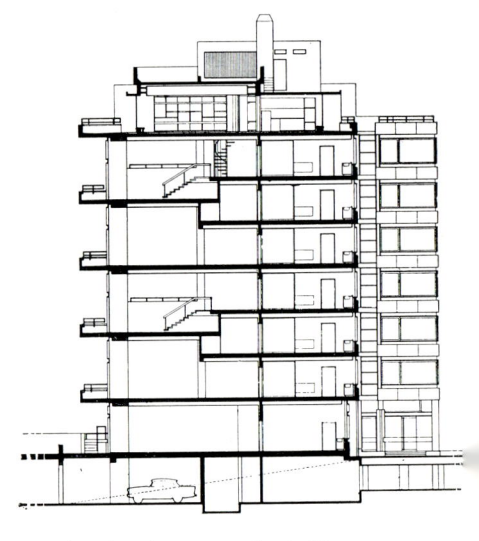

Section showing one-and-a-half storey living rooms. Facing page: view of the same side.

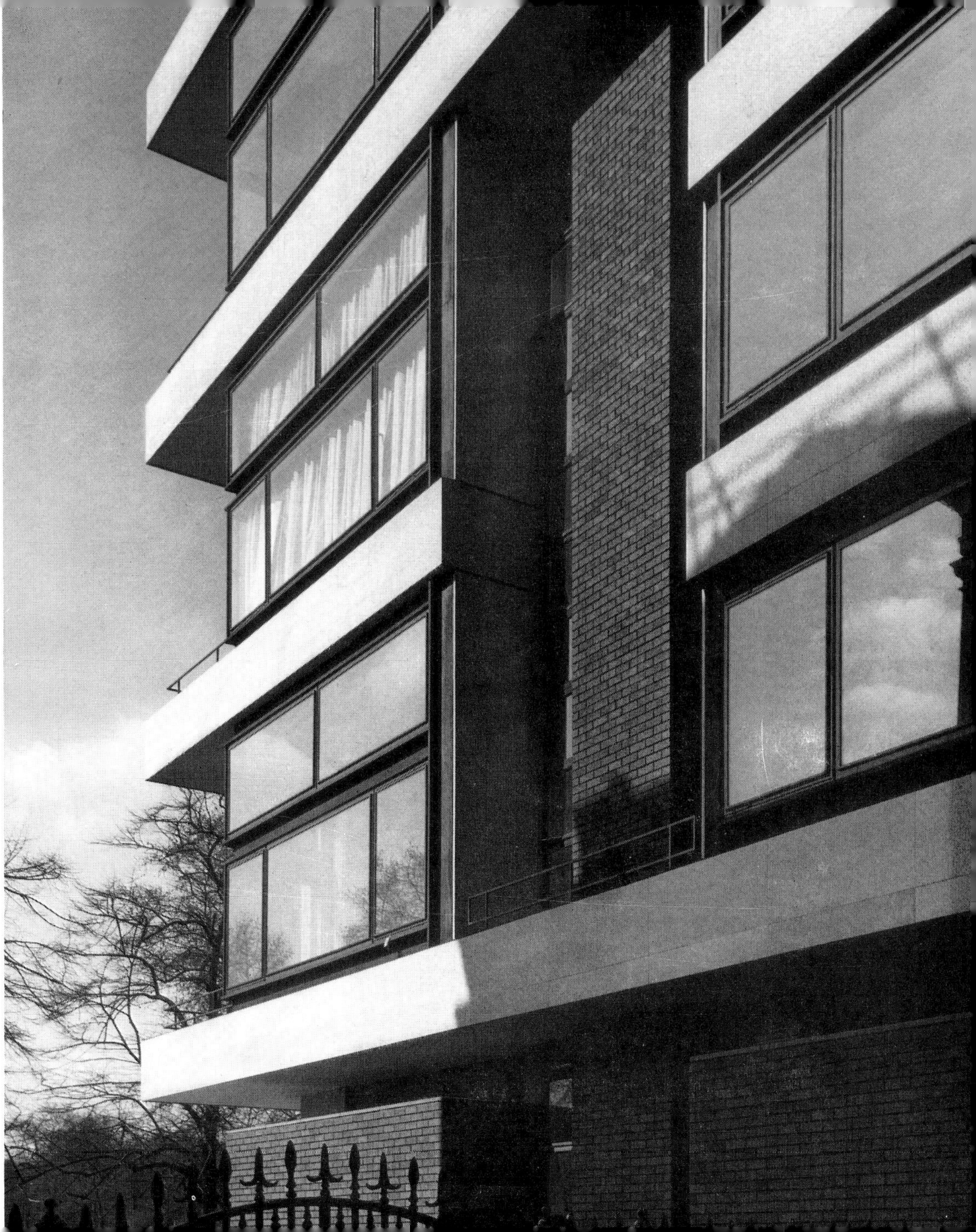

Factory at Bryn Mawr, Wales
Architects' Co-Partnership

Factory at Blumberg, Germany
Egon Eiermann

For a movement officially committed to industrialisation, modern architecture has contributed awfully little to the progress of the modern factory. Most of the best or most celebrated examples have been the work of engineers like Albert Kahn in the US, or Sir Owen Williams in Britain. It cannot be that there is no distinctive contribution that an architect can make, but often the architect's contribution seems distinctive in the dubious sense as well as the good. In the well-known rubber factory at Bryn Mawr—one of the first major pieces of post-war British architecture—the mark of architecture is seen as much in the dated conception of the fashiony, undulating roofs of the ancillary structures as in the grand, and still convincing, central conception of the nine clustered domes covering the main workspaces—one of the most impressive interiors in Britain since St Paul's.

But the darling of recent architect-designed factories, and rightly so since it seems to resist the corrosions of time and fickle fashion better than any other, is the little textile plant at Blumberg in the Black Forest, designed by Egon Eiermann (who was co-designer also of the German Pavilion at the Brussels Exhibition of 1958).

Blumberg's basic attraction lies in having all the modest attributes of industrial architecture to an almost immodest degree; the immodesty lying in the acute visual skill with which they are handled. The main weaving shed has a steel frame and corrugated asbestos cladding; so have thousands of other factories, but they don't have Blumberg's carefully worked out system of external framing and uninterrupted bands of cladding—ponder

Albert Kahn's office contributed an immense quantity of sound, clean, businesslike and sometimes inspired factory buildings to the U.S. automobile industry in the twenties and thirties, and became an exemplar for enlightened industrialists all over the world. Sir Owen Williams's factory for Messrs Boots at Beeston, Notts, was succeeded by a series of other exemplary structures, such as the Peckham Health Centre, that helped to build him an impressive reputation—now somewhat diminished by his rather unimpressive work on the M1 motorway.

Bryn Mawr was designed by ACP—Architects' Co-Partnership—one of a number of post-war attempts to found egalitarian organisations (cf TAC, The Architects' Collaborative, in the U.S.) without any figurehead to act as the focus for an architectural cult of personality.

Facing page: top: air view of Bryn Mawr. Bottom: Blumberg, with boiler house in right foreground.

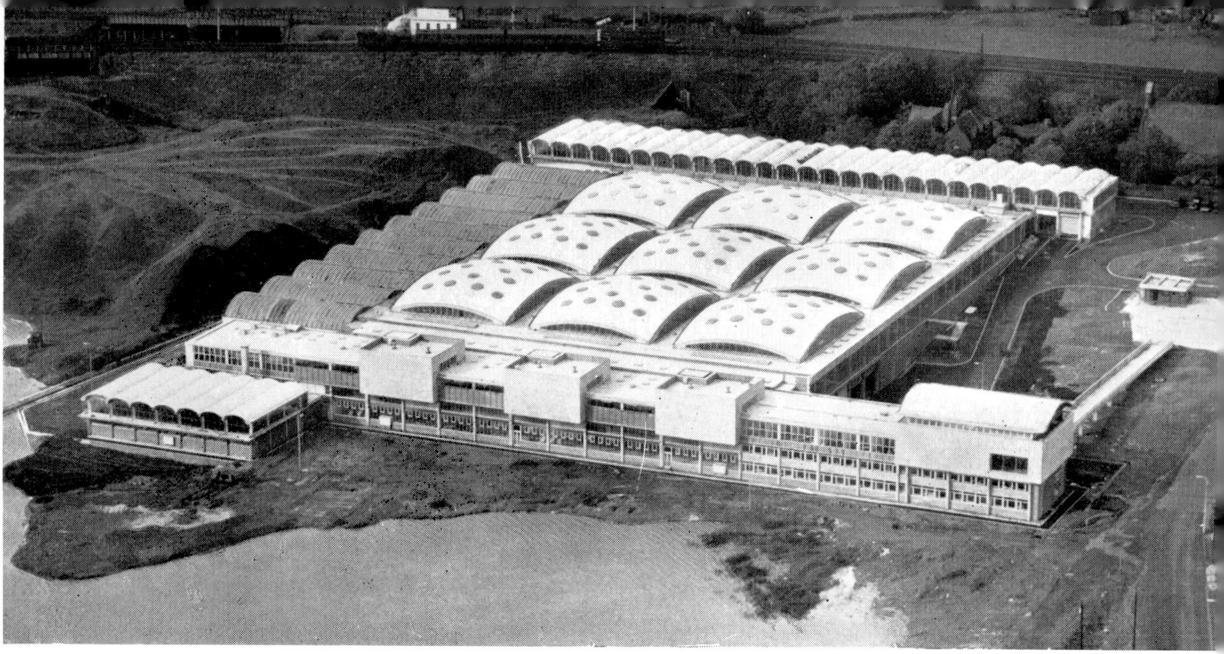

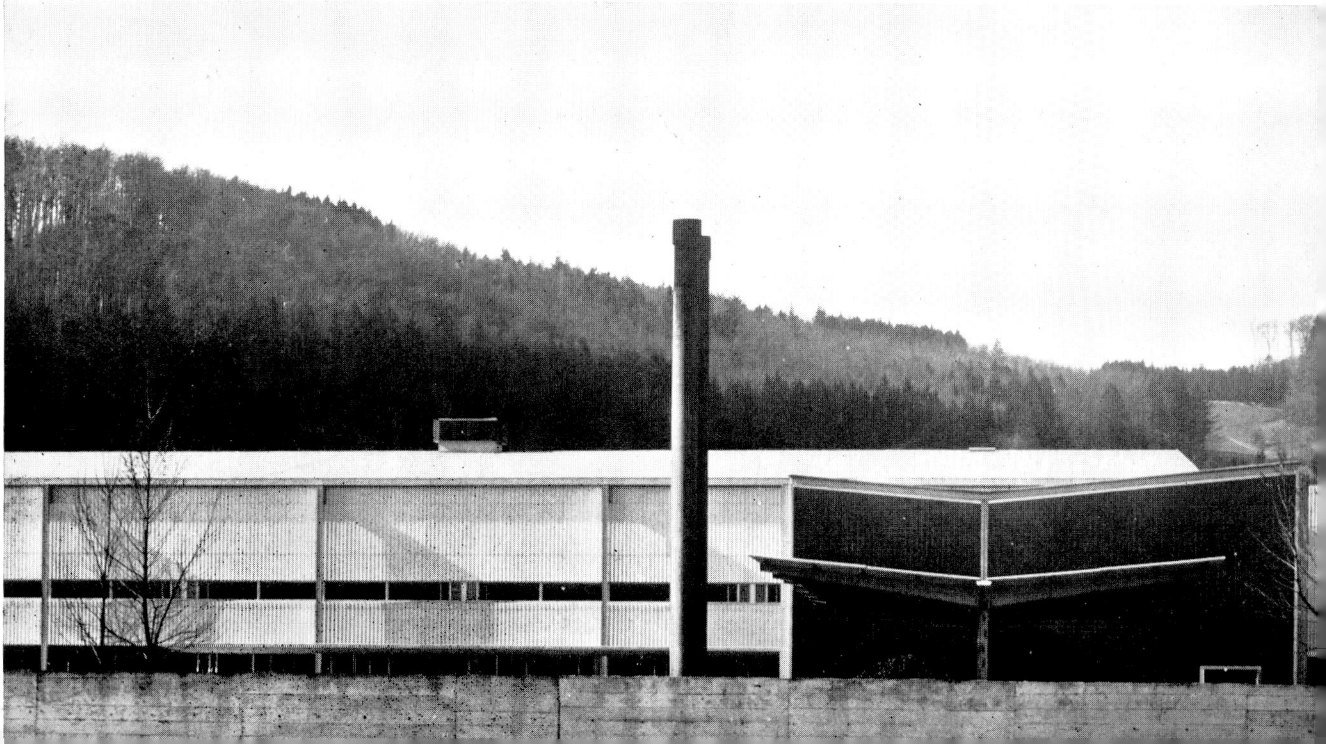

this building carefully and you will begin to see the difference between mere utilitarian construction and inspired functionalist architecture. Equally, the boiler-house is an exercise in the machine aesthetic, so beautifully detailed and proportioned that it is almost in the Mies van der Rohe class—though, inevitably, there isn't the spare money on an industrial commission to support the ultimate refinements that Mies normally demands of a design. Even so, Blumberg comes as close as dammit to that ideal of eloquent reticence that so many functionalists saw as the aim of modern architecture: is this to be attributed in any way to the fact that Eiermann cut his teeth, in design, on stage sets?

The Ford House, Aurora, Illinois
Bruce Goff

To many thinking men, Frank Lloyd Wright was never the all-American architect of his own image of himself. He never appeared as much at ease in the real America as in the America of some splendid Usonian dream, and—in some curious ways—he trailed a whiff of the European *grand-maître* behind him; his following was like a German *Meisterschule* of the high romantic period. Charles Eames, for all his internationalism and lack of Whitmanesque ham, is as American as Campbell Soup. For all his love of things European and Oriental he handles power-tools and catalogued components like a hot-rodder born, and his own house, spare and elegant, square and ineloquent, is American like a Shaker chair or a trestle bridge.

And yet, for my money, the hundred-per cent-pure, good-to-the-last-drop, rolled-from-better-leaf, American architect is Bruce Goff. For him the European mind seeks desperate similes: in his ability to mould the off-cuts of standardised America nearer to heart's desire, he is an even more radical

Above and below: Charles Eames's own house; key letters refer to items in a manufacturer's catalogue of standard units.

Interior of Ford House, showing central balcony.

hot-rodder than Eames; he digs exotic cultures, far-out musics, a-formal arts, so that it is difficult nowadays not to see him as some sort of hipster: consumer-oriented, sensitive to grass-roots public moods, he is the master of the dream-house; without formal academic training, he has devoted much of his life to a Socratic teaching relationship with the young; and though he was once Wright's most fervid admirer and remains a devotee of the immortal memory, there has been no real sign of Wright in his works since the late thirties.

What he has developed since then defies categorisation, and since there is no stylistic consistency running through it, there is no building to point out as typical. The Ford house at Aurora, Illinois, is my personal favourite because I relish the wit with which elements of other structures and other technologies have been re-deployed. The basic bulk of the house is, in form, a sort of squashed-doughnut dome, which has no visible relationship with anyone else's domes, and is built over reclaimed Quonsett (Nissen) hut frames (the army surplus aesthetic!). Some of this framing is skinned over with wood or glass, but some is not, making a kind of close garden occupying a segment equal to almost a quarter of the domed space, and for a large part of the circle, the Quonsett frames are grounded on a dwarf wall of blocks of straight-run channel coal. Flanking quarter domes provide bedroom space, the main dome sheltering a giant living and working room, with a saucer-shaped floor cantilevered out from the central chimney to provide something between a sanctum sanctorum and a tree-house.

All up, the house has the mad logic of so much that happens in the Middle West, and the same irrefutable justifications by local standards. One of the freedoms that Americans don't enjoy as often as they might is the freedom to live in a house designed as if houses had just been invented, but this isn't for want of trying on Goff's part.

Bruce Goff, born in 1904, has existed too long on the margins of fame, designing houses of unclassifiable originality in the Middle West, and suffering periodical discoveries by pundits with axes to grind. He deserves the opportunity to do a big building on a conspicuous site, and thus silence both his critics and his admirers.

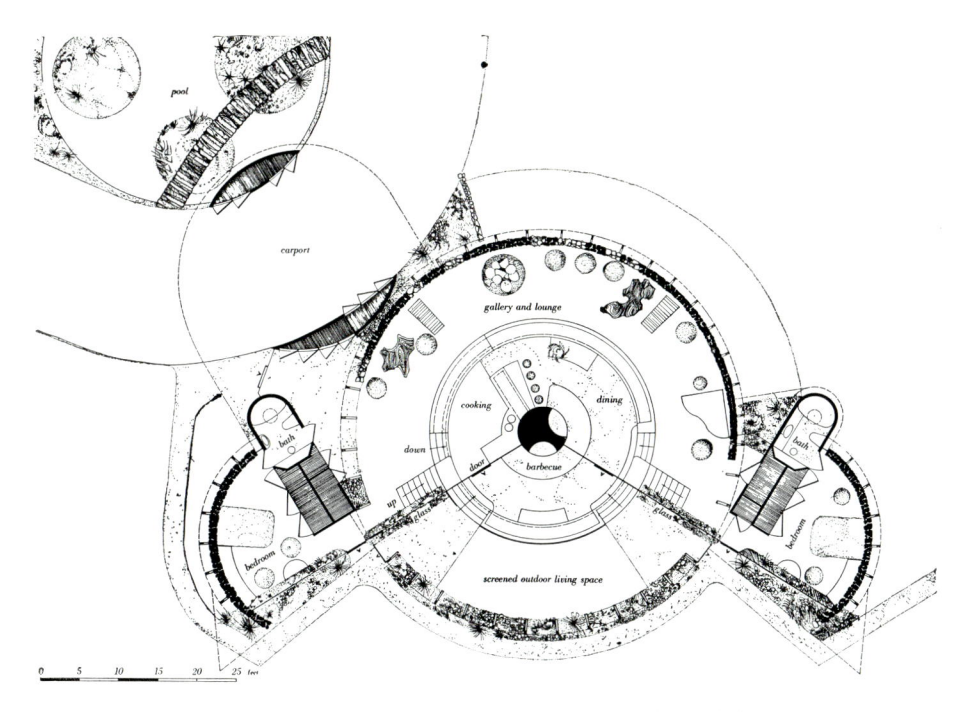

Exterior and plan.

67

Penguin Pool, London Zoo
Lubetkin and Tecton

Not many modern buildings achieve instant popular success, but the Penguin Pool at the London Zoo outstandingly did; and for something like fifteen years it held a unique place as the only playful piece of modern architecture in Britain, until the Festival of 1951. The high popular regard was in some ways unfair to the numerous other first class zoo buildings designed by the Tecton partnership that centred on Berthold Lubetkin for most of the thirties, forties and fifties, yet the esteem is not undeserved. For a long time this oval hole in the ground with its interlocking spiral ramps was out-and-away the least inhibited and least parochial new building in Britain, and it could probably stand examination in its own right as a piece of abstract sculpture of the Anglo-constructivist epoch (the period when Naum Gabo was still working in England). It can also stand up as a pretty crisp piece of concrete engineering for its period; those ramps, though small, must impose some curious twisting loads on their points of anchorage, and are reputed to be practically solid steel reinforcing with a thin cover of concrete. But chiefly, and permanently, the Penguin Pool stands up by reason of its entire aptness to its subject matter and purpose. To the best possible advantage it exhibits the pompous-ridiculous antics of the penguins to the human race whose pompous-ridiculous behaviour the penguins unwittingly ape. In honour of their unconscious mockery, the penguins were flattered with a rather better building than was available to most English human beings of the period. There must be some moral in this.

Berthold Lubetkin's involvement with modern architecture goes back to the Revolutionary years in Russia (where he was born in 1901) and in the late twenties he was one of those strolling Soviet talents, like Ehrenburg or Mayakowsky. He settled in England in 1930. The Tecton partnership, which lasted in one form or another until almost the end of the fifties, served as the training ground for a large proportion of two successive generations of British modernists.

Below and facing page: Penguin Pool.

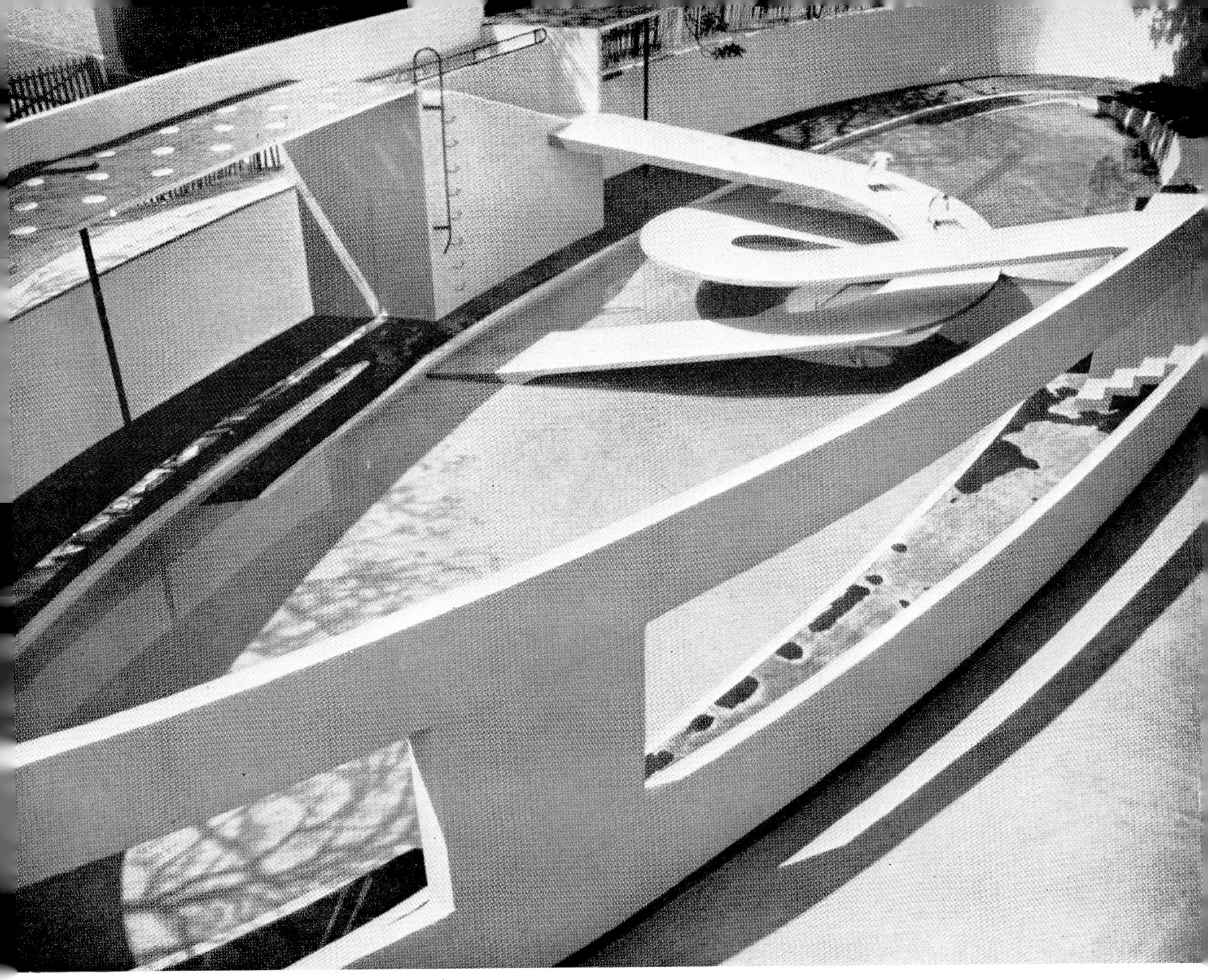

Town Hall, Kurashiki, Japan

Kenzo Tange

One of the most heartening proofs of the continuing vitality of modern architecture is the way Japanese architects have not gone the expected way. Western pundits, critics and informed circles generally had the forward path for Japanese architecture mapped out as a confluence of the native *Sukiya* tradition (informal, black-and-white in the manner of the Katsura Palace) and the Mondriaan wing of European abstract art; the outcome was expected to be something like Mies van der Rohe, and they had even picked the architect who was going to do it; Junzo Sakakura, designer of the sweet and elegant Japanese pavilion at the Paris exhibition of 1937.

It is with real relief that one reports that everybody was wrong, and that Sakakura and his fine-drawn architecture have been trampled underfoot in the stampede to create the real Japanese modern architecture, under the undoubted leadership of Kenzo Tange, who has established himself in half-a-dozen years as one of the world's outstanding architects. Tange's architecture, most eloquently summed up in the Town Hall he designed for Kurashiki, under the enlightened patronage of the Ohara clan, is an architecture of enormous mass, fortress-like solidity, aggressively three-dimensional plasticity. Where the West had expected steel to be used as the equivalent of the slender wooden posts of the *Sukiya* tradition, Tange uses concrete beams as the equivalents of the tree-trunk columns and thundering wooden bracketting of Japanese monumental architecture.

The town hall stands on a ponderous concrete chassis raised on substantial, no-nonsense columns that batter (i.e. taper) inwards towards the top, like the lower walls of some *shogun* fortress. The longer side-beams of this chassis erupt at the ends in two sub-beams, like the ends of some planking system, and the same sort of device, but protruding in both directions and

The small poetic figure of Kenzo Tange, born 1913, has become increasingly familiar around the world as his growing fame causes him to be invited hither and yon. His output is not yet large; its power lies in its ability to combine a convincing primitivism with an almost Futurist view of city planning which, however, has only been expressed in unexecuted projects so far.

interlocking, happens at the corners of the roof slab. In between, the main walls are apparently built up of horizontal concrete planks (some of them omitted to make windows) which collide and interlock at the corners of the block in a manner that says 'log-cabin' in any language. The originality of all this is so striking and so exciting that it is difficult to believe that Tange has arrived at it in a matter of five years from his prim, square, Mieso-Corbusian city hall for Tokyo.

Whatever Mies had to contribute to Tange's style is buried and forgotten now, but the Corbusian inspiration shows through even at Kurashiki. The council chamber has been fairly described as Ronchamp-inside-out, or a floating cocoon within the structure of the building. The slope of its ceiling becomes the rake of the ramped seating of a complementary outdoor auditorium on

Kurashiki town hall; the auditorium on the roof is just visible.

the roof, and this contributes an irregular diagonal element to the silhouette, in contrast to the square block below, much as Le Corbusier often uses roof-top irregularities to set off the standard grids of his façades.

But the entrance hall reveals a positively meta-Corbusian style. The stairwell is dark, overscale. The stair ascends in straight flights, left-handed with a half-landing, cantilevered out from walls that are roughly shutter-patterned exposed concrete, relieved—if that is the word—by window openings that are like nothing so much as mediaeval firing-slits. The effect has been called Piranesian, which is justifiable as long as the term is only applied to the lighting, the spatial play. But there is nothing of Piranesi or his inflated classicism about any element that one could actually touch with the hand. These, as we now begin to see, are the inevitable result of a union of French rationalist thinking about concrete as a manner of building in post and beams (Tange has studied with Le Corbusier), and a Japanese manner of thinking of architecture as the massive combination of heroically scaled horizontals and uprights. The result transcends both, and gives an architecture whose reciprocal effect on the West may be sensational. For, with the appearance of Tange, Japanese architecture ceases to be a colonial export from Europe, and becomes an independent national style in its own very emphatic right.

Laboratories in Philadelphia
Louis Kahn

It is not subtlety or musicianship that makes a popular song, but a good gimmick or punch-line in every verse. So, too, with a building that becomes the rage of the hour—whatever professional craft and architectural skill Louis Kahn may have invested in every part of the Richards Medical Laboratories in Phila-

Entrance hall.

delphia, its uncontrollable success depends on just two simple and superficial things: its picturesque silhouette of clustered towers, and the fact that those towers are mostly for services. It is not easy to say which of these is the more important consideration, because they appear to have run as closely together in Kahn's mind as in that of his admiring public.

Taken in bulk, this busy assemblage of expressively articulated vertical masses and comparatively fragile looking horizontal truss-work, complex and irregular in plan, is a reaction against the smooth anonymity of the Mies tradition, that would have wrapped up the whole project in one exquisite crystalline box, and this reaction has clearly chimed in with the increasingly picturesque mood of the post-Brutalist world (Kahn is one of the Brutalists' favourite architects). But, in addition, this is a building whose functions demand a formidable array of mechanical services (to clear off toxic atmospheres from the laboratories) and Kahn has expressed this with an equally formidable array of brick monoliths crowding closely about the glass boxes with the laboratories in them. Nothing could make more clear or more dramatic Kahn's concept of the servant spaces (towers) and the served spaces (laboratories), and to a profession increasingly concerned with the problem of packing mechanical services—bigger and more complex every year—into or around their designs, the Philadelphia towers were triumphant proof that the solution of the services problem could be monumental architecture. One point remained to be resolved however: was it architecturally honest to make something so very monumental ('Duct-henge' was the ribald estimate) out of anything so transient and changeable as services, here today and obsolete tomorrow?

Louis Kahn, Estonian born in 1901, and now the great luminary of the 'Philadelphia School' of architects, has been a late-emerging talent, unappreciated until the decline of dogmatic Functionalism set younger architects in search of traditional values in architecture. He first attained world notice with his Yale art gallery of 1955, and has since become the object of a fanatical cult of personality.

Laboratories at Philadelphia, seen over the roofs of earlier buildings.

Como

Works of Giuseppe Terragni

Como and the Italian lakes have a reputation for producing masons and architects. They contributed major talents to the middle ages and the early Baroque, and another gaggle of Comacines produced Italy's only serious contribution to the first phase of modern architecture. Antonio Sant'Elia, one of the bright stars of the Futurist epoch, was born in Como and built no buildings, but his drawings, his example, his legend were the inspiration of the Italian 'rationalist' architecture of the twenties and thirties. Though he anathematised monuments and monumentality, his name appears on a gigantic monument on the shores of Lake Como that is unmistakably Santelian in style. It was worked up, from a number of his sketches for other things, by Enrico Prampolini and Giuseppe Terragni, whose career and death in the second World War were an almost exact repeat of Sant'Elia's a generation earlier, except that Terragni built buildings, nearly all of them in Como.

They are a remarkable group; the education of an architect in five structures. First the Monument to Sant'Elia and the dead of the First World War, a stark, symmetrical composition of abstract forms, a white dipylon braced by canted buttresses rising from a base of grey stone—not yet modern, but a drastically purged classicism. Then *Novocomum*, the block of flats behind the Fascist stadium. It preserves the symmetry, but everything else is harsh and deliberate modernism borrowed from Berlin and Bolshevik Moscow. Nothing could be more period and dated than the edgy alternation of bull-nosed and sharp-arrised corners that contribute most of the visible 'architecture' on the exterior. Then comes maturity with a rush: the Casa del Fascio, one of the most brilliant formal exercises of the thirties. Functionally, it simply stacks floors of offices around the sides of an internal court, the front opening up into an exposed

Terragni was born in 1904, and died in 1943 after experiences on the Russian front which permanently damaged his mind. While the quality of his work makes him a figure of undoubted world standing, his equivocal relationship to the Mussolini regime also makes him a figure of controversy—one can safely say, however, that his was a great talent ruined by Fascism.

Below: Monument to the Fallen. Facing page, top: *Novocomum*; bottom: Casa del Fascio.

FEDERAZIONE
P.C.I.
PARTITO
SOCIALISTA
ITALIANO
LAVORATORI ITALIANI
DEMOCRAZIA
CRISTIANA
E.N.A.L.

structural frame. The interior is no more nor less offensive than other Italian interiors of the period; it has the air of being made of materials at once pretentiously shoddy and incredibly permanent, but the front, seen across the piazza outside the cathedral and theatre, is stunning—a monumental diagram of the rules of *divina proporzione* immortalised in marble. For those who believe that modern architecture is still subject to the grand old rules, it is proof that the rules are still valid. For those who believe that modern architecture has to do with social progress, it is the machine aesthetic at its most heartlessly elegant. But, outside the official Fascist context, Terragni is not heartless. The Casa Giuliani-Frigerio, nearer the lake again, is a blithely fashionable exercise in the style of Rietveld's Schröder House, with external flyaway sun-screens and balcony frames. It is the father of several thousand cut-price variants in post-war Italian suburbs, but its freshness is quite untarnished by its nasty progeny. The fifth and most humane of his significant buildings in Como, is an infant school, the Asilo Sant'Elia, the most fairy-godfatherly compliment ever paid to the young by a modern architect. Here, Terragni's passion for open frames and courtyard plans produces a delicate environment of airy, lightly-shaded spaces and framed views of greenery beyond, unaffected (though not without its formalisms) and still, to my mind, the best school built in Italy in this century.

Facing page, top: Casa Giuliana-Frigerio. This page and bottom of facing page: Asilo Sant'Elia

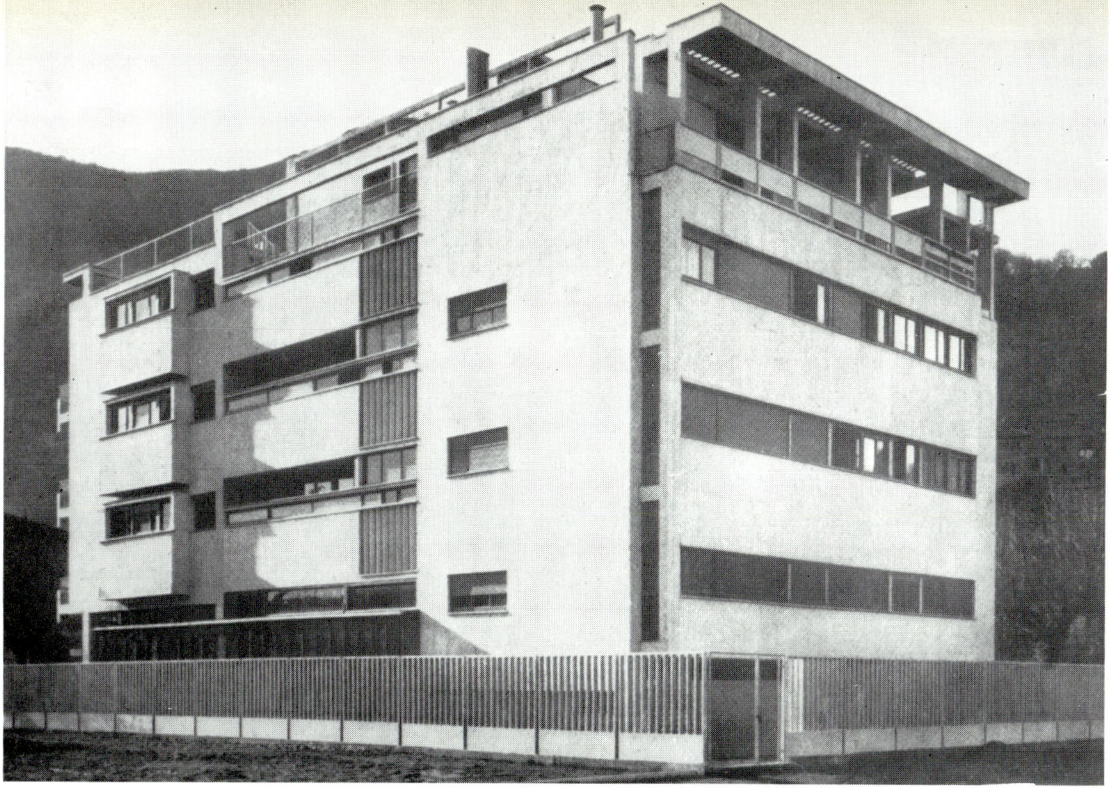

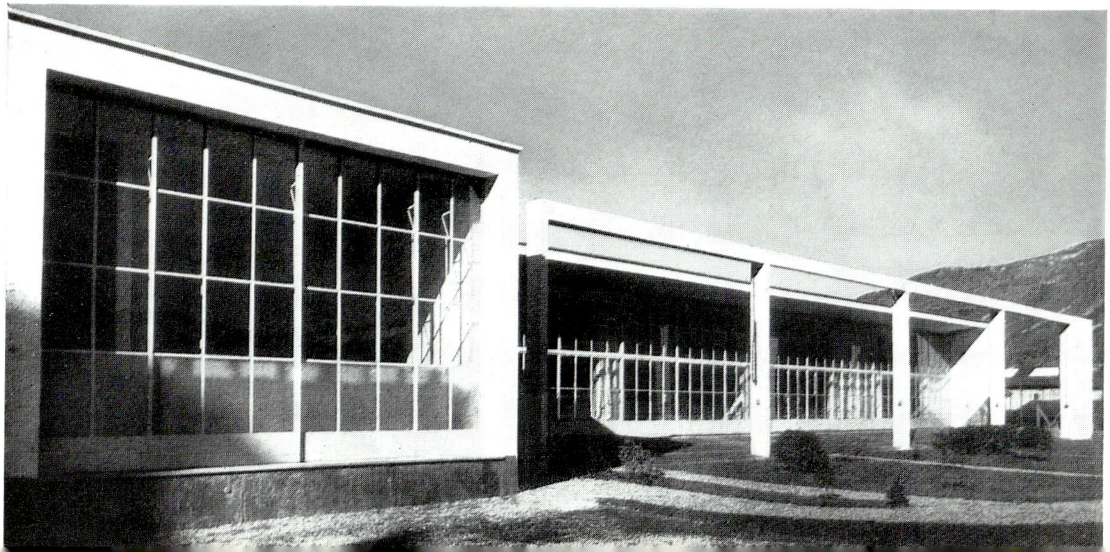

Casa del Girasole, Rome
Luigi Moretti
House on the Zattere, Venice
Ignazio Gardella

Some buildings are embarrassingly modern: they become tests of taste, like the Casa del Girasole, which was much argued over in the early fifties. Its architect, though a man of formidable culture and intellect, is not quite trusted in some architectural circles, and his doubtful position, as expressed in his work, enables him to throw revealing light into skeleton-haunted cupboards. Long before the eruption of Neoliberty (the Art Nouveau revival) called the progressive aims of modern Italian architecture into question, the Girasole had made them look pretty dubious. What goes on inside it is in no way modern; routine Roman apartments, planned along a corridor, and composed into a block raised above the street by a basement full of servants and services, as in all Italy back to the Quattrocento. But the exterior is unmistakably modern, *Italian* modern, like the most serious work of his Milanese contemporaries. Standing wide over its narrow basement, it is as modern as the Pavillon Suisse standing wide over its pilotis.

If this were just window-dressing, a veneer of modernity, the Girasole could be dismissed and conscience salved. But its modernity is not just skin-deep. Moretti has cogently argued that the split of the façade follows inexorably from the divided plan, and having thus made modern-type architecture out of bourgeois degenerate planning, he rubs in the message with wit. The façade is made to look like a false front, yet the apparently useless extensions of the walls beyond the limits of the rooms are to provide roll-away space for the shutters, and although the concrete frame of the building is nowhere exposed, Moretti strip-teases the limbs of classical statuary among the rustication of the lower walls, as if secret caryatids were holding it all up.

Above, and top of facing page: Casa del Girasole. Bottom: House on the Zattere.

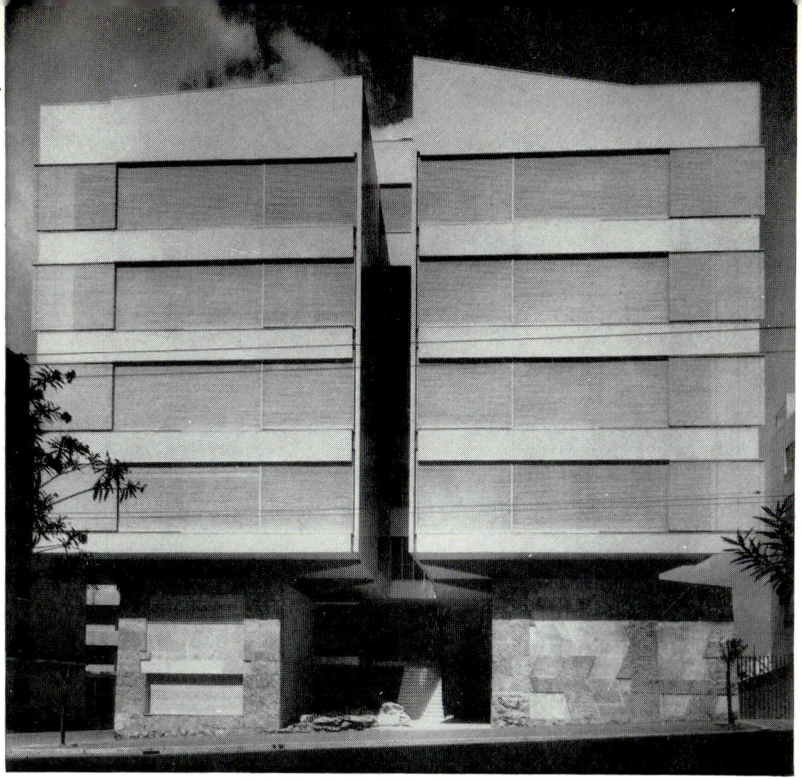

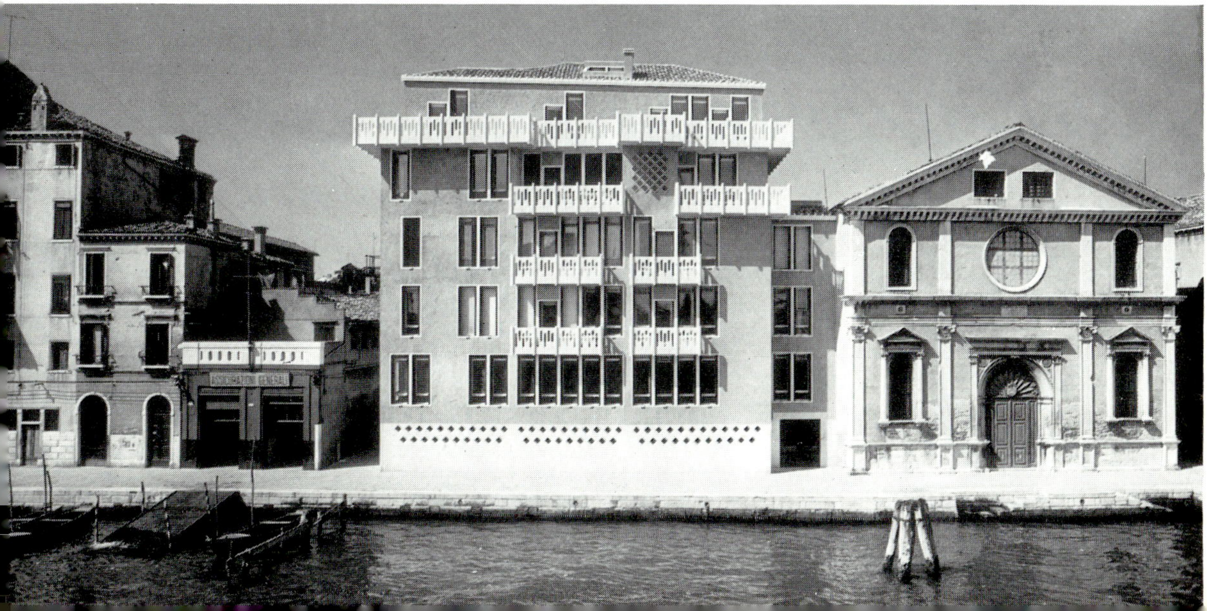

'A joke,' we all said, 'all right as long as it doesn't go any farther' and Moretti has not pursued it. Yet something very like it was done, for quite different ends, in Venice by Ignazio Gardella. His apartment house on the Zattere degli Incurabili is an extraordinarily witty capriccio of modern and vernacular themes that add up to a new building which looks so much like a conversion job that it vanishes into the Venetian townscape the moment your attention wanders. It is fancy-dress architecture, certainly, but the very manner of its disappearance is proof that the dressing-up has not been done for the usual reasons of historical cowardice. Very tricky. . . .

The Robie House, Chicago
Frank Lloyd Wright

All his long life Frank Lloyd Wright remained, as the saying went, the greatest living master of the nineteenth century; his admiration of craftsmanship long outlived his mechanistic enthusiasms of around 1900, and many of his most salutary designs of the twentieth century can best be regarded as final versions of nineteenth-century themes. The Robie House is one such: its importance as a mentor to the domestic architects of the present century is beyond question, but it is hardly modern architecture at all in some lights. Its affinities are with a tradition of *de luxe* suburban villas that reaches right back into the Victorian epoch and beyond.

The Modernist admirers of the Robie House have emphasised its abstract and spatial qualities, the great oversailing roofs, east-west below, north-south above; and the massive megalith of the central chimney that binds all together and makes sense of the rather vague relationship between the expanses of roof and the plans of the rooms below them. But, at close range on the sidewalk, the visitor is much more conscious of the fact that he is

The life of Frank Lloyd Wright is becoming the best known of all architectural biographies. Its long span—he lived from 1869 until 1959 and just failed to reach ninety—covered more than half the history of the USA, and embraced sundry periods of his own professional activity. Of these the first notable one ran from 1893, when he set up in independent practice, until 1910 when he left Chicago for Berlin under a cloud. The next did not begin until after 1930 when his fortunes as an architect at last began to revive, and he then enjoyed nearly thirty years of floodlit senescence, of which the first two decades produced some of the best buildings of his whole career, and the last five years some of the silliest projects ever conceived by an old man, anywhere.

confronted with such familiar impedimenta of suburbia as dwarf-walls, giant flower vases, shrubs and leaded lights. This image of a familiar, tarnished and sentimental dream can be so overwhelming that the house that launched the modern movement almost single-handed, tends to vanish, momentarily, behind a haze of old associations and resentments.

    Yet it is through these very details that the originality of the Robie House begins to re-assert itself as one looks. The brickwork, before the mortar was mistakenly re-pointed flush with the brick surface, had horizontally raked joints (the mortar set back about half an inch from the brick face) so that whereas there was brick, there was also an obsessive horizontal interest, to which the long continuous planes of the stone cappings to the walls also contribute, as also do the squat spreading forms of those exaggerated flower vases. Before you have lifted your eyes

Robie House. The flower vases are at each end of the low wall.

from the garden wall you are deeply involved with the themes of horizontality and overhang.

Even the diamond tracery of the leaded lights has the diamonds wider than they are high, making a sprawling, horizontal, glass-consuming pattern of arrow-head forms that echo the arrow-head plan of the ends of the main rooms. The decoration is, indeed, everywhere congruent with the house, from the smallest detail to the total effect of the bulk form, pushing out horizontally, invading and surrounding space.

The men who brushed aside its superficial suburbanities as irrelevant, in order to concentrate on its play of planes in space, knew it only from photographs—except for the one man who built the only European version that is even remotely comparable in quality. Rob van t'Hoff had worked briefly in Wright's office, knew the Robie House at first hand and drew his Dutch colleagues' attention to it. His version, the celebrated villa at Huis ter Heide, outside Utrecht, is the exact half-way-house between the American inspiration and the final European realisation of a new architecture. Its complex and niggling interior denies the magisterial expansiveness of Wright's planning, but its exterior denies also his romantic surfaces. This cleaned-up version of Robie, crisp and clean, prim and symmetrical, is a travesty—as J. J. P. Oud recognised—of Wright's *Americänische High-Life*, but it was a necessary step in turning Wright's nineteenth-century conclusion into a twentieth-century beginning.

Schocken Store, Stuttgart
Eric Mendelsohn

That which the gods seek to destroy, they first frighten with near misses. The Schocken store survived the pulverisation-bombing of central Stuttgart by inches and stood up as a symbol of commercial persistence among the ruins; remained to become an

Right: leaded lights of Robie House.
Below: villa at Huis ter Heide.

object of pilgrimage for a generation re-discovering its period and its designer, Eric Mendelsohn, and—just when it was beginning to be recognised as one of the true masterpieces of the twenties—its owners and Stuttgart's megalomaniac traffic-planners had it pulled down.

Mendelsohn has never been an easy architect to assess: his practice (largely commercial while he stayed in Germany) his patrons (Jewish) his doctrine (structural expressionism) and his vocabulary of rounded and rhetorical forms, are all rather alien to the mainstream of the modern movement, even though derived from similar sources (Wright, machinery, structural technique and so forth). All this would have been no bother had Mendelsohn been a negligible architect, but he was not. He was brilliant, perhaps a sort of genius, and he gave to department-store design the same kind of radical authority as Gropius could give to institutional buildings. His Columbushaus in Berlin, or his second Schocken store in Chemnitz, may seem more immediately convincing in photographs, but to encounter the Stuttgart version in the original was to see just what he had to offer. Many architects have paid lip-service to the excitement of outdoor advertising, but Mendelsohn could really do it, he had the mind for *reklame*. Schocken's non-advertising side-walls were model exercises in unobtrusive but well-architected functionalism, but the main façade on the Eberhard-Ludwigstrasse was something else again. Its ground floor was, in sheer acreage of plate glass, competitive with any of its contemporaries, but above this the brickwork of the side-walls slashed crisply across the glazing in a powerful pattern of horizontal stripes of solid and void to make a stunning background for giant three-dimensional cut-out lettering spelling SCHOCKEN (later altered to an underscaled *Kaufhaus Merkur*). At its southern end the facade was closed by a projecting semicircular stair-tower, the full height of the façade and entirely satisfying as a solid volume. But it was not a solid, and between projecting cornice-strips as closely

Mendelsohn died in 1953, the first major talent of the generation of the eighties (born 1887) to leave the architectural scene. The rise of the Nazis having made his position impossible in Germany; he came first to England, where his major work was the Delawarr Pavilion at Bexhill, and later went to Israel and the USA

Facing page: Schocken store, showing stair tower and main façade.

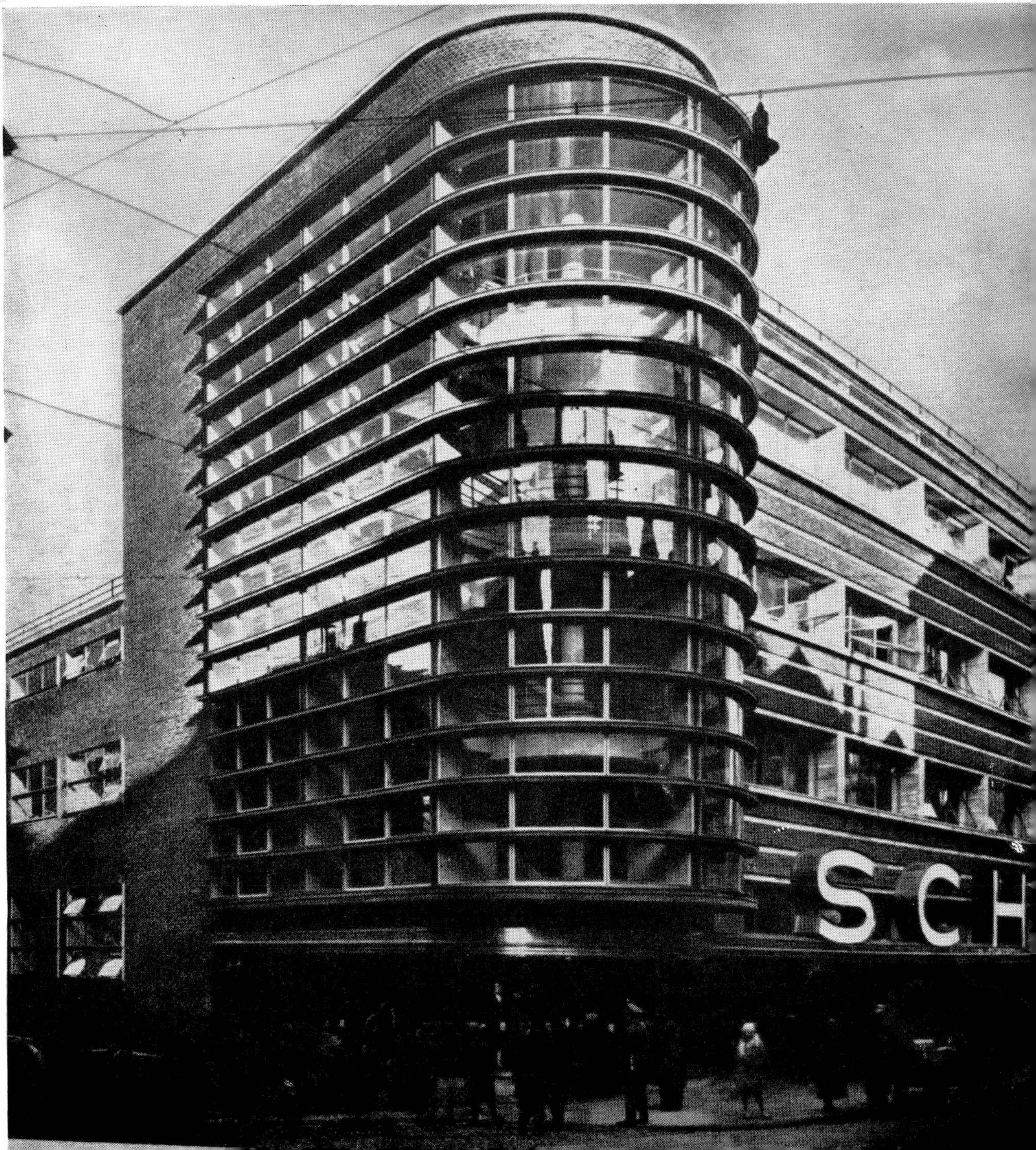
SCH

spaced as the fins on a motorcycle cylinder, one glimpsed through to shoppers on the stairs within. Or with a change in one's position, or the fall of light, one got reflection instead of transparency, and suddenly saw the buildings on one's own side of the road, mirrored in extreme vertical distortion, transformed into ogres' castles and baroque cathedrals. It was everything eye-catching that advertising ought to be, but without cheapening the architecture; it was modernism with the popular touch, without cheapening the architect, and that—in sum—is what made Mendelsohn so hard to take for so long.

Johnson Wax Company Buildings, Racine, Wisconsin
Frank Lloyd Wright

Worn down by the Master's own continuous rhetoric of earth, sky, rock, wood and agricultural virtue, most of us have come to accept a mythological picture of Frank Lloyd Wright as a sort of super-peasant, a primitive dolmen-builder suffused in bardic Welsh light. Certainly the tribal encampment that he created under the hill at Phoenix, Arizona, and called Taliesin West, is the masterpiece of Romantic primitivism in modern architecture, but all through his career run buildings of conspicuous machine-age sophistication, such as the Guggenheim Museum, and the king and queen of this persuasion are the Johnson Wax offices and their attendant laboratory tower.

The offices are near-enough contemporary with Taliesin West and could hardly be less like it. To the outside world, Johnson Wax presents blank brick walls, unpierced by windows, and rounded off with bull-nosed corners. But at the cornice (for want of a better word) the walls come to life with a glistening bulge of glass, for all the world like the chromium edge-trim of some primitive piece of Detroit car-styling. In functional fact, this glass trim is a piled-up system of parallel glass tubing that

Johnson Wax buildings, general view. Facing page: top: pre-war group with glass cornice; below: interiors with lily-pad roofs.

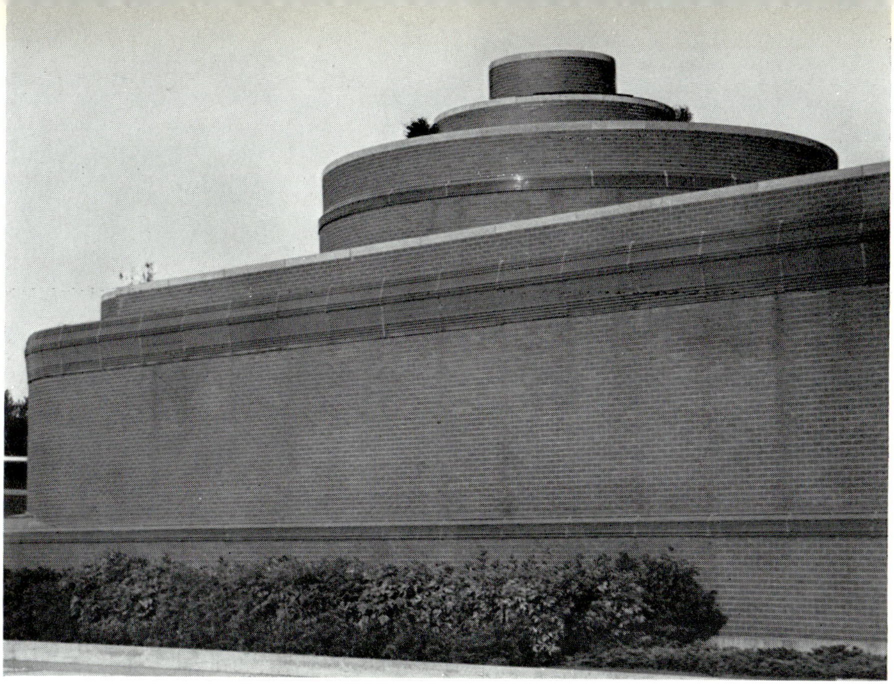

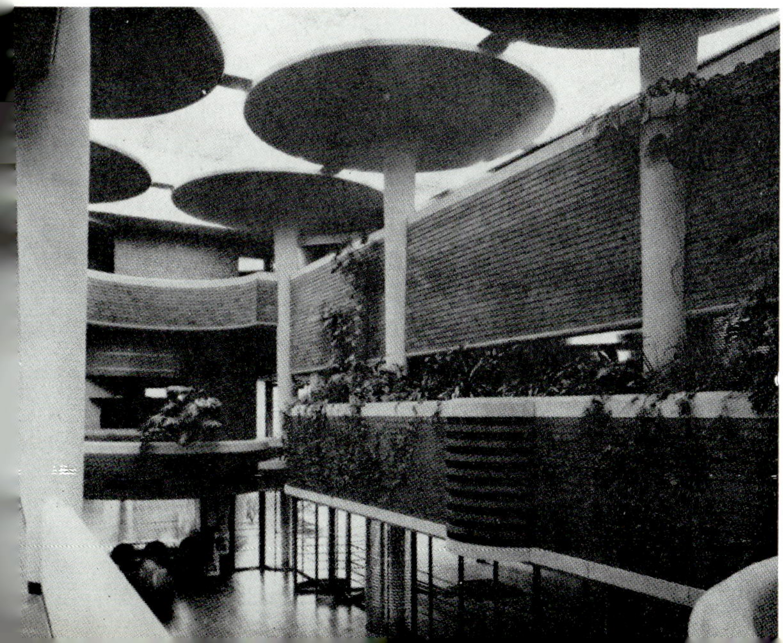

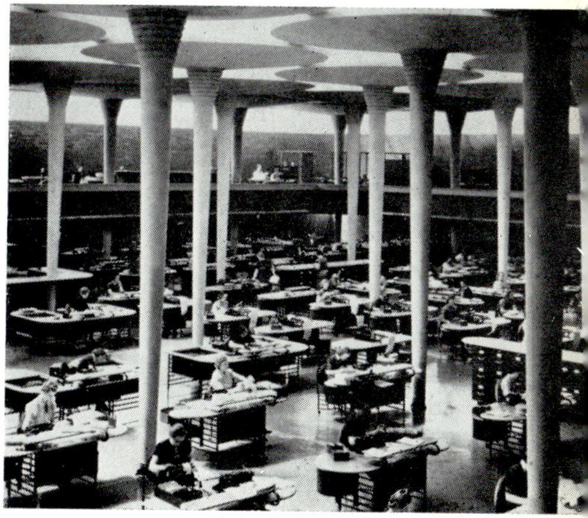

acts as a light diffuser, spreading light into the interior (and part of a membrane of similar tubes that roofs over most of the habitable interior space). Function notwithstanding, its appearance on the exterior gives a very strong sense of industrial styling, and the bridge unit that connects the different parts of the complex continues this theme by looking very like the chain-guard or similar part of some machine-tool: it is part of the image of progressive industrialism being worked up in the same period by the pioneer U S industrial designers like Norman Bel Geddes and Raymond Loewy. Through *their* efforts, in particular, it began to look like the beginnings of an all-American architecture in the buildings of the New York World's Fair of 1939. It came to nothing (for a variety of historically compelling reasons such as the war) and Johnson Wax alone survives as a monument to the style.

It will always be remembered for the interior of the general office, a fantastic fish-tank roofed in concrete lily-pads and the membrane of translucent glass. It was not Wright's first office, and he had earlier shown his preference for deep, top-lit workspaces fitted out with office-equipment purpose-designed by himself. At Racine, the desks follow the bull-nosed aesthetic of the exterior, and have semi-circular ends, while the structural lily-pads on stems run all through the building, supporting not only gossamer glass ceilings, but also quite massive structures such as over-bridges.

When he came back to Johnson Wax, after the war, to design the laboratory tower, he decided to build the whole structure around a single lily-pad stem, and cocoon it in glass tubes—even round the bull-nosed corners. Alternating round and square work-floors are speared on a single central column like meat and vegetables on a *kebab* skewer. The circular floors are slightly smaller than the square ones and do not quite reach the outer skin which consists, as one sees it from outside, of alternating bands of brickwork and glass tubing on a square plan.

Although the corners are still snubbed off, as on the earlier block, the effect of the tall, banded tower is no longer primitive industrial design, but vaguely pharmaceutical or even electronic. The image of industrial progress had shifted and Wright with it, keeping an accurate finger on the pulse of technology even when pleading loudest for 'the natural house'.

Post-war laboratory tower.

Unité d'Habitation, Marseilles
Le Corbusier

The building for which a generation of architects waited almost a decade to give them a vital sign—the sign under which the real post-war architecture was to be born—was Le Corbusier's *Unité d'Habitation* at Marseilles. Few projects have so accurately summed up the aspirations of their day so aptly, few can have so fully satisfied a body of disciples while disappointing their leader. Corb's disappointment stemmed from the fact that he intended to build a whole suburb in a cluster of such blocks, but politics and economics thwarted him in this particular case (and have yet to give him a proper chance anywhere else he has tried). The satisfaction of his followers stemmed from the fact that it was the largest building completed as he had designed it (his U N project was being progressively coarsened and diluted) and because it showed that he was still on the move, still making architecture anew.

The design, famously, called for a single compact rectangular block (descended directly from the *Pavillon Suisse*) containing apartments (mostly duplexes) and certain day-to-day social services such as shops and crèches subsumed within the block. The scale was immense—over 300 apartments—but was halved visually by expressing the double height of the duplexes by single openings on the outside, and putting the whole thing up on legs two storeys high (but looking only one). But something else happened to the scale in the course of design: originally conceived in terms of steel construction, the project had to be reconsidered from the ground up when the usual post-war shortages required concrete to be used instead. Somewhere in the consequent delays and re-appraisals, the Master re-appraised also the aesthetics of reinforced concrete, abandoning the pathetic fallacy that this was a smooth precise machine-aesthetic material, and once more enquiring after its true nature. Instead of putting

Below: section through the Unité, showing double-height living-rooms. Facing page: exterior.

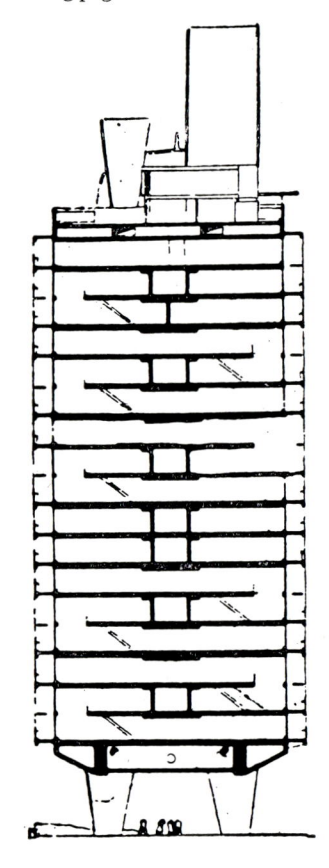

up a delayed pre-war building, he produced the first truly post-war one, monumental, not mechanistic, in the scale of all its parts.

Beginning with the legs—Le Corbusier's original concept of pilotis, as he called them, had been slim smooth cylindrical columns: at Marseilles they were massive pachydermatous stumps, tapering towards the foot and patterned all over with the impress of the plank-work of the shuttering in which they had been cast. So was all other concrete that had been poured and cast directly in place, and as the eyes of a delighted generation scanned the immense façades they saw concrete expressed by an architect almost for the first time as what it was, a moulded plastic material that could not exist without form-work in which to cast it. Further, Corb was visibly possessed of an aesthetic capable of dealing with this revelation: the surfaces showed the accidents of grain and knot in the unplaned planks that had been used; but the arrangement of those planks was no accident, and they had been laid in patterns as carefully as those of rusticated stone-work or a tiled floor. The first of the 'more crumbly aesthetics' of the fifties had been born.

This exterior was beyond dispute—there was some argument about what went on inside. Not about the two floors of social facilities half-way up, but about the flats themselves and the access to them. Each duplex apartment occupied the full thickness of the block on one floor, and half of it on the other, the deep narrow apartments being Chinese-puzzled in pairs around the central corridors that occurred on every third floor. Although both ends of the long floor of each apartment reached the outside air, even with a two-storey opening for the two-storey living-room, it was at the expense of a plan that was little better than a Bibby cabin, and the bedrooms in the long 'tail' of the flat were like a railway van. The access corridors, in turn, though dignified by their creator with the name *rues intérieures* were, after all, little better than very long corridors without natural lighting. Characteristically, disciples who would hear no criticism of the master were soon at work improving both concepts, the improved apartment appearing in the LCC's Loughborough Road flats, the improved *rue intérieure* being partially exteriorised in the street decks of Park Hill at Sheffield.

But there were no second thoughts about the roof: even the rather gratuitous running track round its perimeter could be forgiven, forgotten in the state of aesthetic euphoria induced by this fantastic collection of functional megaliths, looking as if the

Most people seem to know that Le Corbusier was born Charles Edouard Jeanneret in la Chaux de Fonds, Switzerland; the year was 1888. It soon became apparent that his talents were too big for little Chaux, but they proved not yet big enough to survive in Paris, Vienna or Berlin, and he did not finally settle for France and Paris until 1917. He remained Jeanneret for his painting and art criticism for some years, but became Le Corbusier for architectural writing in 1920, and for architecture when he began to build again in 1923. He had an established reputation by 1928, and has never looked back since, except to re-style his autobiography from time to time in order to keep his image in line with the needs of the hour.

Facing page: top: roof structures; bottom left: pilotis showing marks of shuttering; right: living room of flat, looking inwards.

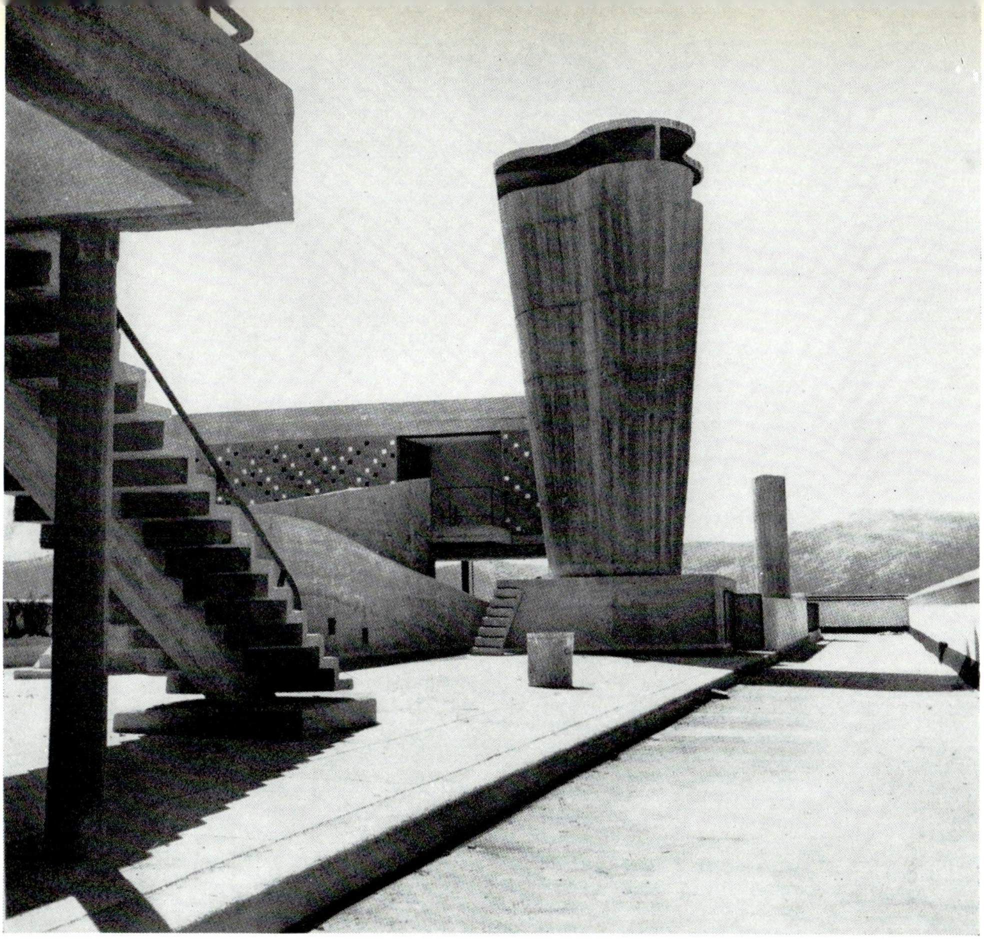

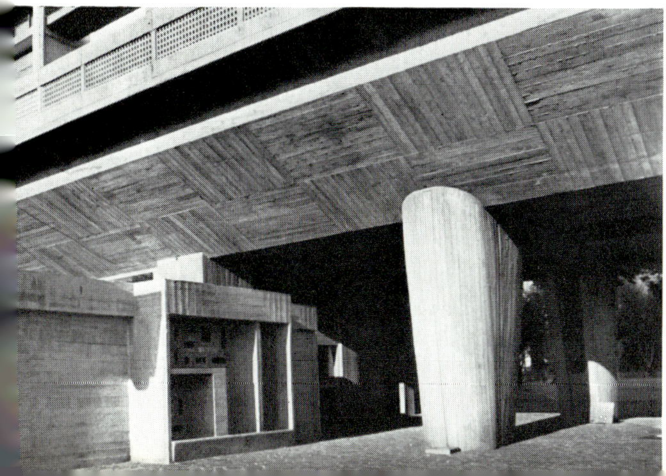

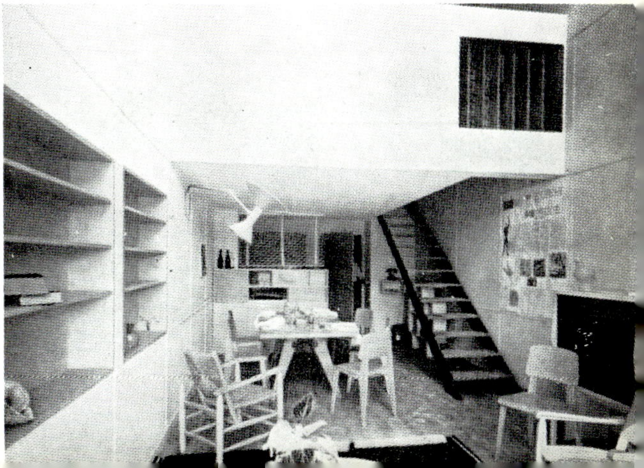

children of giants had left their educational toys on top of the toy-chest. Seen against stunning views of mountain, sea and sky, the powerful shapes of these ventilators, lift-motor houses, play sculptures, platforms and stairs modelled by the sun, distilled for a generation the essence of 'the Mediterranean thing' and gave substance, triumphantly, to Le Corbuiser's most famous definition of architecture— 'the cunning, correct and magnificent play of volumes brought together in light'.

The Seagram Building, New York
Philip Johnson and Mies van der Rohe

Lever House, New York
Gordon Bunshaft of Skidmore, Owings and Merrill

Few architectural trialogues can be as fascinating, or as inscrutable, as that between the Seagram Building and the Racquet Club, facing one another across Park Avenue, and Lever House, oblique from Seagram but flanking the Racquet Club. The club is a most expert exercise in Beaux-Arts expertise by McKim, Meade and White, the American partnership who showed the French in the nineties that the Ecole des Beaux-Arts could be beaten at its own game of brilliant cliché-mongering. The Racquet Club is an *exercice de style* carried off with a stylishness that almost makes up for the emptiness of the style, and a skill in resolving visual problems that still strikes a chord in the architects of today.

Indeed, this trialogue is a discourse upon style in the grandest manner, in which the club puts down a basic proposition of traditional skill, and the other two discourse upon it in modern terms, derived from New York's first true prism, the UN Secretariat. UN was a European dream, the glass tower set between city and water, planted in a townscape where skyscrapers

Facing page: Seagram on left, Lever House on right. The Racquet Club is the building facing Seagram, with an arcaded top storey.

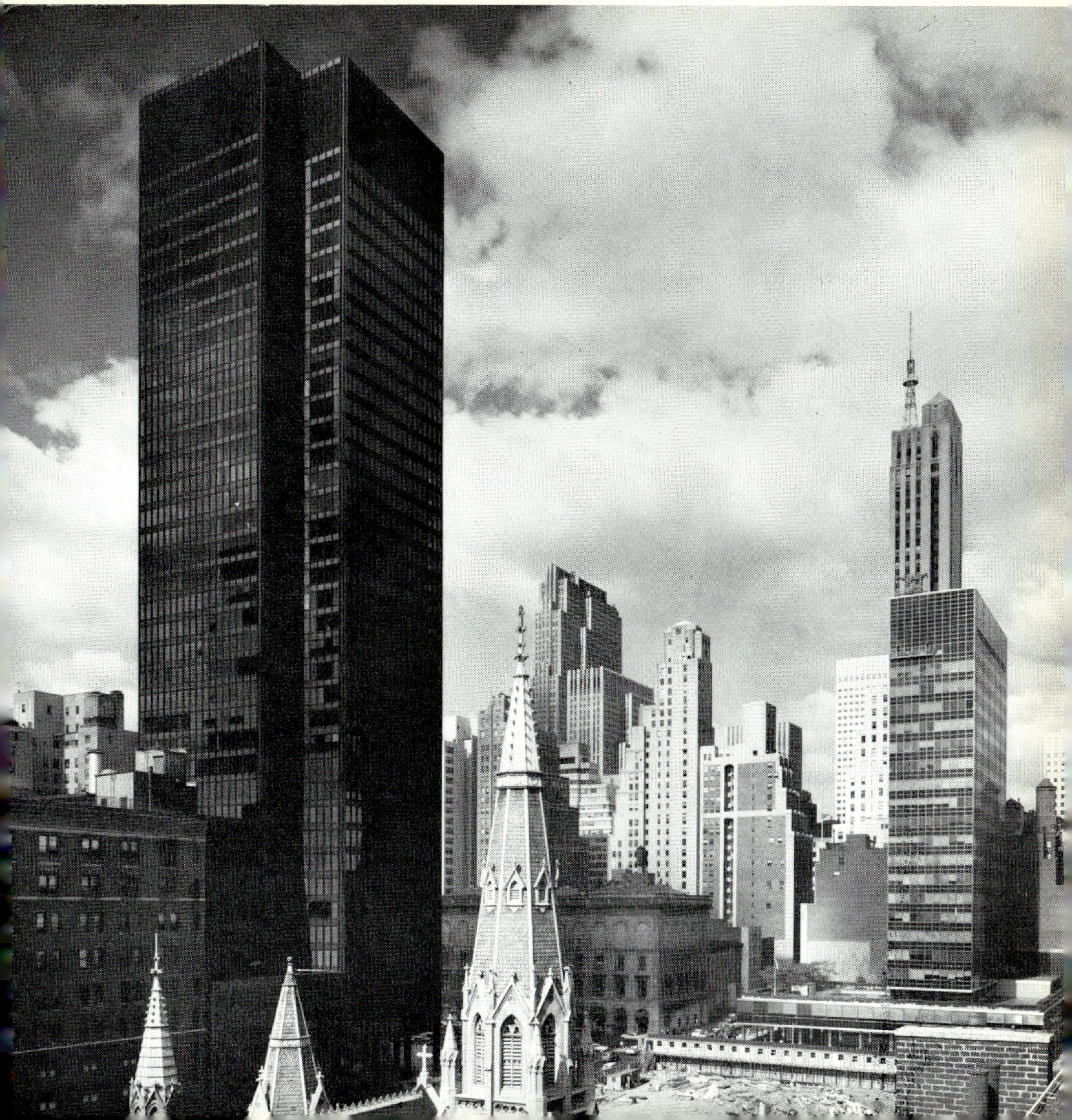

are not a dream but a dirty commercial reality. The contrast between the ideal and the real set off a brisk discussion on the aesthetics of the skyscraper in New York, and Lever and Seagram are the two most authoritative statements made, in built fact, in that discussion.

Gordon Bunshaft, the most brilliant designer to practice under the S O M umbrella, clearly set out to Americanise the European dream represented by U N, by imparting a dash of the puritanical —Lever is glazed all round, U N only on the main façades— and more conspicuously public-spirited: Lever is flanked by a little piazza 'dedicated to the public use'. Unwittingly or clairvoyantly, Bunshaft built a monument to an America whose existence could barely be sensed at the time: Eisenhower America, grey-flannel-suit America, with Madison Avenue literally only a block away. Its smoothly elegant solution was typically a compromise between two great creative ideas—Le Corbusier's vision of the tall slab with auxiliary structures at its foot, and Mies van der Rohe's vision of the all-glass tower. It gave architectural expression to an age just as the age was being born, and while the age lasted, or its standards persisted, Lever House was an uncontrollable success, imitated and sometimes understood all over the Americanised world, and one of the sights of New York.

But it was not what many observers believed it to be at the time, the last word in glass boxes. Over in Chicago, Mies van der Rohe was steadily developing his aesthetic (or was it a structural *rationale*?) of refined purity and rectilinear structural expression to a point of seeming logic well beyond the craftsmanly compromise of Lever House, and in the mid-fifties— rather suddenly, following some brisk internal intrigue among the Bronfman (Seagram) clan—Mies van der Rohe and his most devoted follower, Philip Johnson, found themselves designing an office block almost opposite Lever House.

But not dead opposite, and the first acknowledgement that the

Skidmore, Owings and Merrill have only become the life, soul and epitome of big business architecture since the beginning of the fifties. An immense and reliable design-organisation even before that date, they still needed the undoubted talents of Gordon Bunshaft (born 1904) who joined the firm in 1946, to propel them to the forefront of the US and world scenes. With Lever House, in 1952, SOM and Bunshaft made a permanent mark, and entered on a career that transcended the limitations of big business architecture with such works as the US Air Force Academy at Colorado Springs.

The partnership of Mies van der Rohe and Philip Johnson on the Seagram building was the consummation of a master/pupil relationship. Johnson, born in 1906, was a late-comer to architecture, and did not begin to train, let alone practice, until he was almost forty. Before that, however, he had been one of the most active propagandists of modern architecture in the US, and helped to create the atmosphere in which it became feasible for Mies (born in Aachen in 1888) to leave Germany in 1937 and make a fresh career in America. One of Johnson's first independent works was the famous glass house at New Canaan, in avowed emulation of the steel-and-glass style that Mies had been working up in Chicago. Since then their paths have drifted apart, stylistically, but their mutual regard seems as high as ever.

Right: Lever House.

Seagram makes to any of its neighbours is to the Racquet Club. Standing back a little haughtily from the pavement, it takes care to share the same axis as the club, each standing symmetrically about the entrances that exactly face one another. This kind of formal good manners is Old World (not to say Olde Worlde) and quite un-American, and at every turn the Seagram reveals a kind of sophistication, an approach to urbanism, that has more in common with the Europe-oriented architecture directly in front of it, than with Bunshaft's unmistakably All-American Lever House standing catty-corner to the right. Lever stands well up to the pavement, but its slab is shoulder-on to the road. Seagram stands back, and front-on to the Avenue. Lever plays up glassiness, transparency and reflection, but Seagram, surprisingly, does not, emphasising instead the solidity of its block form, using a tinted glass that is darker and browner than Lever's, and bronze mullions that stick out from the façade as positively as pilasters, whereas the aluminium glazing-bars at Lever barely ripple the surface, while the actual proportion of the tall narrow windows above the bronze spandrel panels (Lever has glass spandrels) recalls the fenestration of ancient palazzi.

Perhaps Seagram will settle in with age, but at present the discourse upon style is carried on with a distinct European accent, and Bunshaft's building, as native as an automat, can hardly get a word in edgeways.

Facing page: top: Seagram and its forecourt; bottom: Lever House and its piazza.

Pirelli Tower, Milan

Gio Ponti and associates, Pierluigi Nervi and associates

Italy's contribution to post-war architecture has been equivocal, and the critical assessment of many of her new buildings an uneasy exercise. One among the many difficulties has been the brilliant and formally perverse way in which Italian architects have underlined the falsity of the old equation between classical

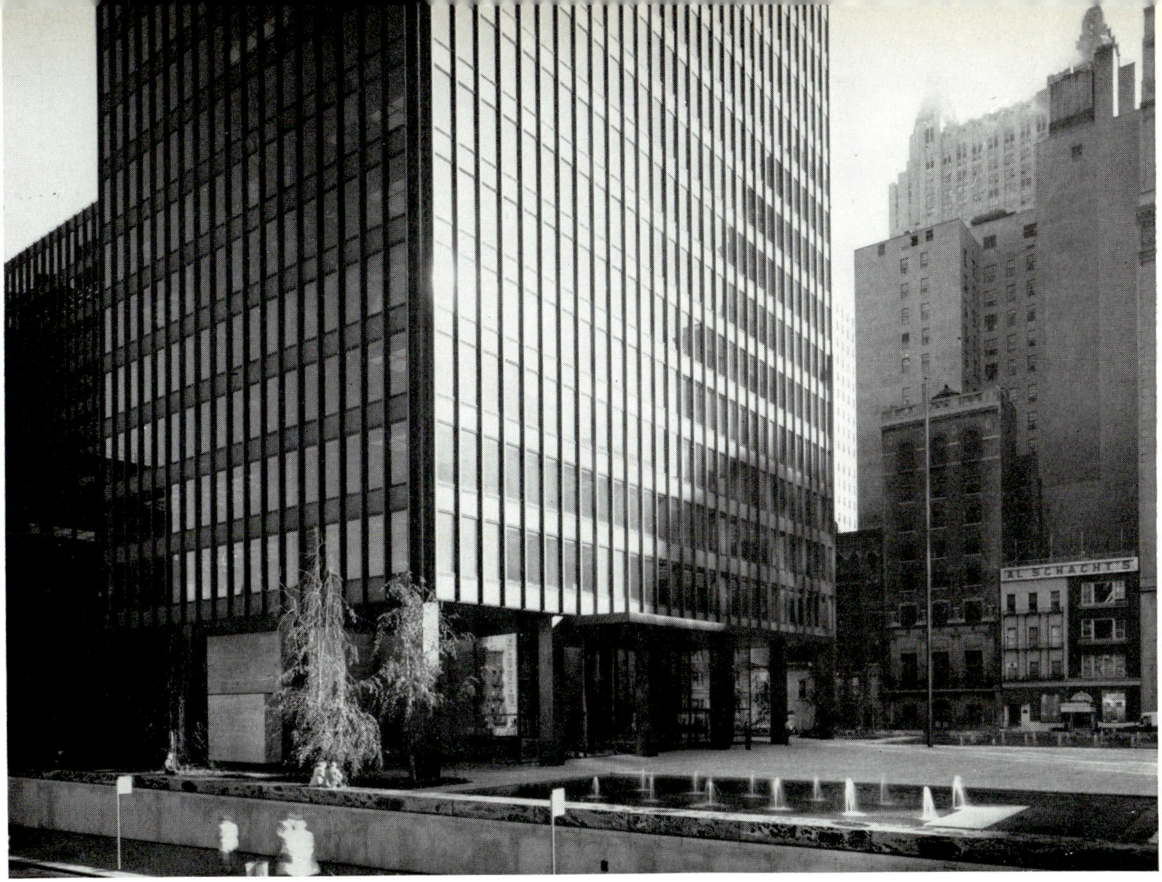
AL SCHACHT'S

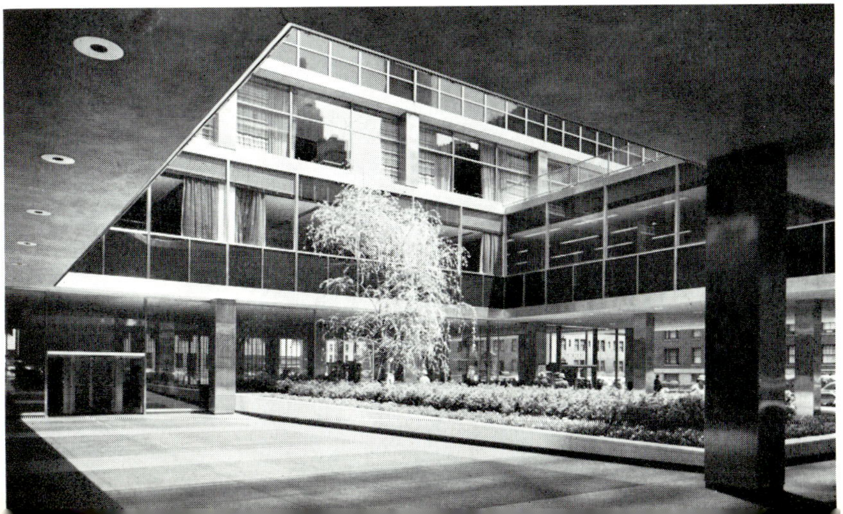

purity and machine technology that has bedevilled critics and architects alike since long before Le Corbusier made it eloquent in *Vers une Architecture*. Using traditional craft and pre-technological materials to produce supposedly mechanistic effects of smooth precision, the Italians coincided with Le Corbusier's *beton brut*, in accidentally undermining the symbolic values of the machine aesthetic, and reduced its stern canons to a formalistic game. Through all the resulting chaos and equivocations, Gio Ponti (everybody's favourite idea of an Italian artist-architect) has picked his way with a politician's skill, dashing off one sizzling design after another, many of them elegant trivialities, infuriating his more committed contemporaries. Then in 1959 he emerged as captain of the team that conceived a building that proves him to be more than just an elegant trimmer to the winds of fashion.

The Pirelli tower, flanking the Piazza outside Milan's abominably rhetorical central station, is one of the half-dozen towers of the fifties that matter. It re-states all the Italian formalist equivocations over the machine aesthetic and yet gives that idiom new life as surely as the Seagram building. By one of those coincidences that make history improbable (though not as improbable as those surrounding the inception of the Seagram building) the impeccable structural logic of that phase of Nervi's career came into conjunction with certain formal preoccupations of Ponti's, and the world now has a building that is not formalist in spite of the care given to the study of its form, a tough-minded business building that is not just a rent-box, an advertising symbol that is not just a gimmick—and all this realised in a building that is manifestly a unified, integrated conception, in spite of the hours of sweat and horse-trading around the conference table that must have gone into its design.

The result is a building that looks razor-thin from end-on, and almost is: two main façades bend back to meet one another in plan, but never quite make it because an air-gap runs up the

The reputation of Gio Ponti, born 1892, might well rest on his two beautifully detailed, but rather forbidding office blocks for Montecatini in Milan, but as editor of *Domus*, the monthly magazine of architecture and design, he has also propagated a more general image of Milanese high taste, that his own minor works, from the *Pavoni* coffee machine onwards, have done most to substantiate.

Pierluigi Nervi, born in 1891, was another slow starter in public esteem, and his present high standing may owe more than is generally realised to the brilliant work of the American photographer, George Kidder Smith, who did so much to open the eyes of the world to Italian post-war architecture. Since then, the merits of work like the Unesco assembly hall in Paris, and the Olympic stadia in Rome have been so manifest that Nervi's reputation has needed no outside assistance.

Facing page: the Pirelli Tower.

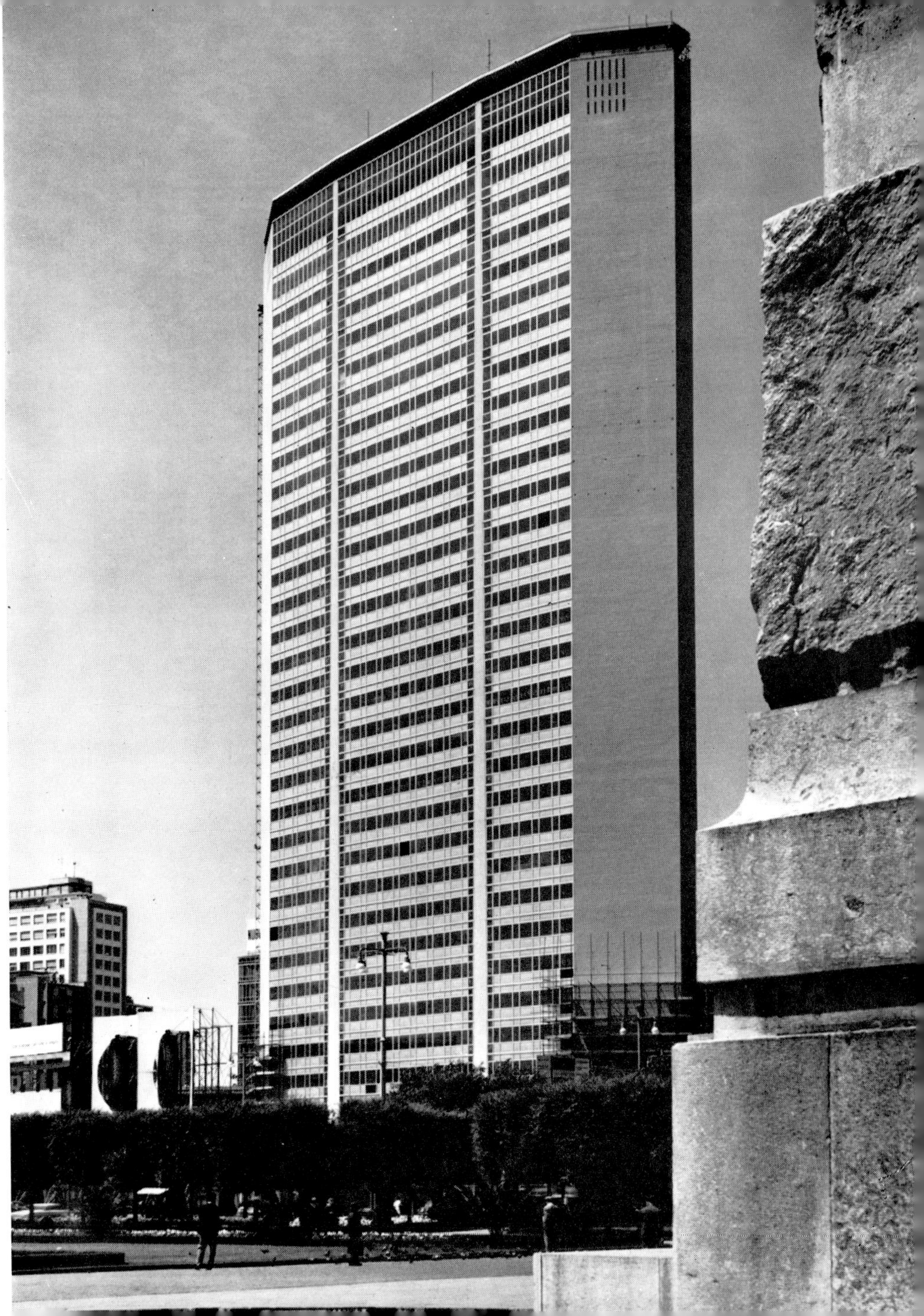

full height of the building just where the cutting-edge of the razor should be. Up the main façade run a pair of slender tapering columns, outward manifestation of Nervi's all-tapering structure within. At the top they carry a flat lid of a roof, but not visibly; the glass wall of the façade stops, and the columns are bent back inside, one floor below the roof, which floats above another air-gap. The three air gaps—down each end and one under the roof—give the tower the air of being a front, a back and a lid, on the point of joining to make a closed box, not yet closed, but for ever aspiring to do so.

It is that aspiration that Ponti wants the observer to see, for the Pirelli, like most great modern buildings, is a statement, a proposition ('slogan', says Ponti). As a counterblast to the endlessness and repetitiveness of curtain-wall architecture, Ponti wanted a Pirelli to be read as a closed form: a *forma finita*. Because it is just on the point of closing, it is read as closed far more securely than if it were finally shut and finished. It may not be a very grandiose ambition to create a building in which a fairly simple formal intention is to be read, but it is quite something to have achieved it in an idiom like that of modern architecture, which has produced so many buildings that will be for ever inscrutable to the man in the street or piazza.

Termini Station, Rome
Eugenio Montuori and associates

There was a time in the middle-fifties when it seemed that Rome railway station was to become one of the wonders of the world. And yet it was only a salvage operation, a smart and democratically tolerable front put on a body that had been conceived and largely built (look at its flank-walls!) in the prissy, neo-classical idiom of the Fascist palaces of Terza Roma, that unfinished Mussolini-inspired townscape in the manner (and mood) of de

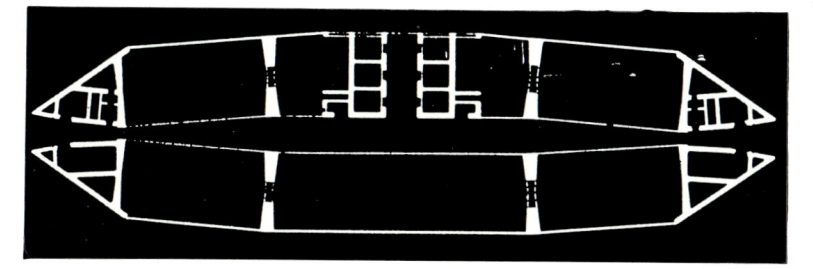

Facing page: vertical section showing the tapering columns. This page: top left: roof space and top of column structure; top right: night view; bottom: plan, showing services in wedge-shaped ends.

Chirico, outside the city. Thousands of tourists and pilgrims arriving in Rome, however, see only a light and spacious cross hall and, beyond it, a giant canopy that waves them on into the Piazza dell'Esedra. It is the only twentieth-century railway station that has achieved the rare feat of looking like a railway station while looking as if it had something to do with the twentieth century.

But the visitor who has hurried through its halls should pause and look back, before he heaves himself into the arms of the Eternal City, because the exterior deserves a second look. To the left, as he views it, a piece of genuine Roman wall has been preserved in a green enclave (a piece of honest respect to Ancient Rome that seems to have been beyond the projectors of the original 'Roman' design) and this serves to spark up the more brightly the modernity of the station itself. The fore edge of the canopy, an immensely long and difficult space that might easily have got filled up with advertising, has been made over to Mirko Basaldella for a sheet aluminium relief that is probably the longest piece of modern art in the world—also the least obtrusive and one of the most effective in doing what it has to do. But it is above this that one perceives the neatest trick of Montuori's design. The long flat wall of the office block that also spans the front from side to side is only five true storeys high and might have looked an insignificant nothing in height, but for the simple expedient of making *two* strips of windows to each floor. The resultant distribution of light, at head and ceiling level, is not as awkward as one might guess, while the gain to the architecture by visually increasing the height of the block, and also the apparent size of the canopy, is the sort of effect that only an Italian, it seems, would have the nerve to try and attain by such means.

Facing page: Rome Station. Top: exterior, with Roman wall on left; bottom: interior of main concourse.

107

Pavillon Suisse, Cité Universitaire, Paris
Le Corbusier

Come to terms with the Pavillon Suisse, and you have come a long way to getting to grips with modern architecture, for it contains much of the basic modern craft that has survived through every change of superficial style; its influence has gone round the world and altered modern architecture for good; and it combines all that is least superficial of both the new and the old in the style.

From the past, it inherits one of the great ideas of the academic tradition, even though it was never made obvious there: this was the conception of a building as an assembly of volumes, each serving a specified function. The idea is as old as architecture, but Le Corbusier here made it eloquent and comprehensible by thinking not of a building, but of separate functional volumes, and designing the building by pushing these volumes together in such a way that their separateness and the fact of their assembly were unmistakable. The main function is to provide living accommodation for Swiss students, and this function is therefore served by the main functional volume, the dormitory. Its identity as a volume is underlined by lifting it off the ground on pilotis, so that one sees at once its actual size and content—the content being expressed by the forty-five room-size windows on the main façade—every square a room, every room a student. Where the pattern is varied at the topmost storey, this is because the content is varied: these are no longer standardised students' rooms.

The other functions are auxiliary and are therefore served by volumes that are obviously accessory to the dormitory: by a stair-tower that, as near as dammit, doesn't actually touch the dormitory block, and by a sprawl of single-storey accommodation at ground level which, because it does not house the same standardised accommodation as the dormitory, breaks away also from

Facing page: Pavillon Suisse.

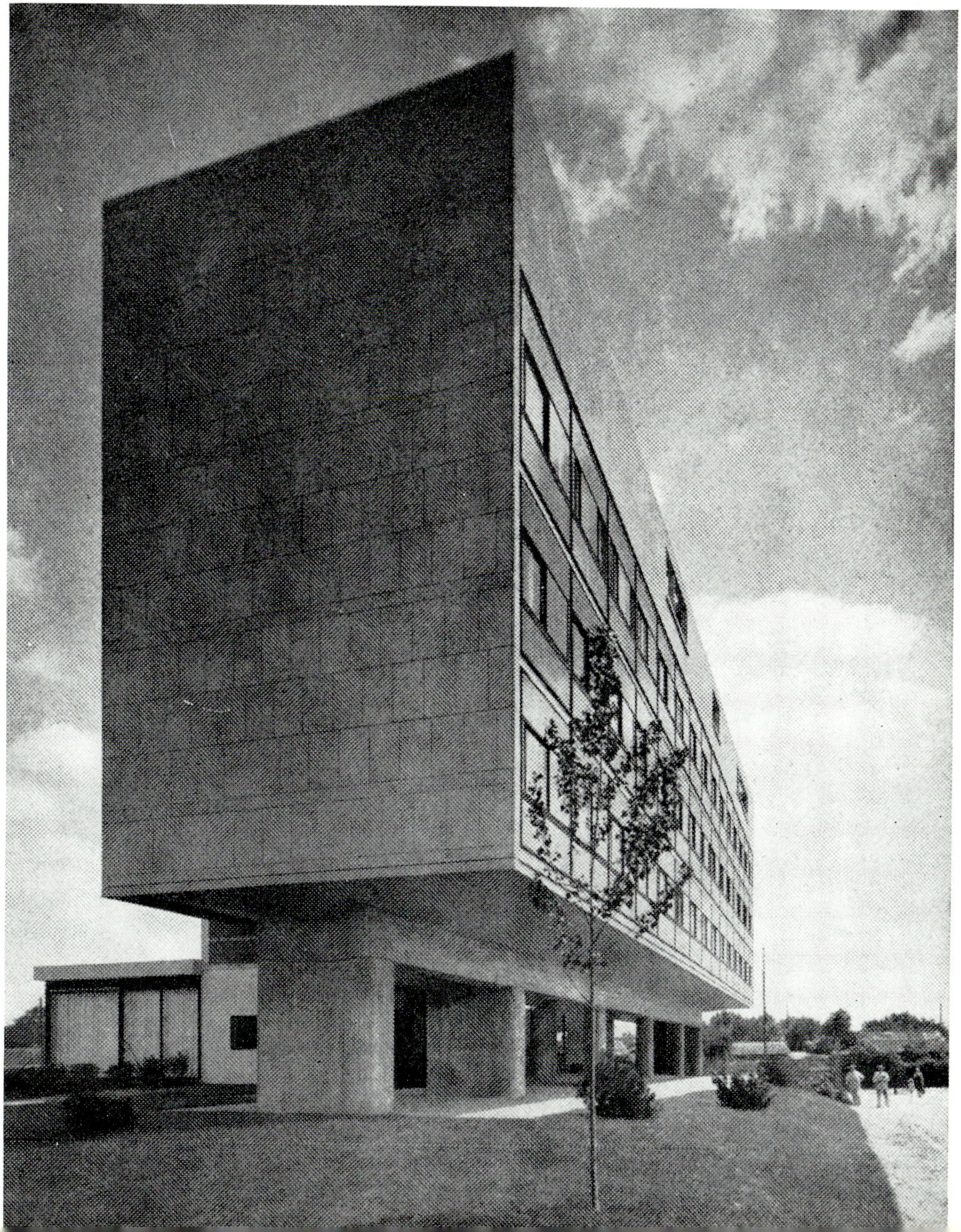

the standardised square geometry of that part. These two auxiliary structures are related to one another by the common feature of a curved wall on the stair-tower and a curved wall on the back of the students' common room, but their difference is at once emphasised by the fact that the staircase wall is of smooth stone slabs, whereas the common-room wall is of highly picturesque random rubble. This systematic alienation of the parts can be seen in one more symptomatic usage, where the porter's lodge, a forward extension of the single-storey structure, edges forward under the chassis of the raised dormitories—it looks suspiciously as if Le Corbusier has only done this in order to leave a gratuitously thin air-gap between the two at a point where a lesser man might have decided there was some structural gain in joining them up. Let no god, says Corb apparently, join what man hath decided to set asunder.

It is difficult to say which is the more compelling here: the brilliant demonstration of a hierarchy of functional parts with their functions carefully discriminated, or the emotive mixture of straight and curved, rough and smooth, romantic and classic —the 'two geometries', it has been called, or 'Corb's surrealism'. The ultimate surrealism of the design becomes most apparent when one realises that he has put his 'rustication' on a wall that does not support any upper storeys (i.e. the common room wall) while the smooth upper storeys, that would traditionally require a rusticated base, stand upon apparent nothingness; the chassis under the dormitories is cut back and rests on a narrow double file of columns under the centre of the block. Yet, even while traditional forms are being surrealistically flouted, the traditional and very French discipline of rational discrimination of functions has been fully honoured in the un-traditional composition of the whole.

The Pavillon Suisse has been described as one of the seminal buildings of the century, and it is true; its progeny are scattered all over the world, and number such distinguished buildings as

Facing page: top: back of stair-tower and common-room; bottom: plan. The dotted line represents the area overhung by the main block.

111

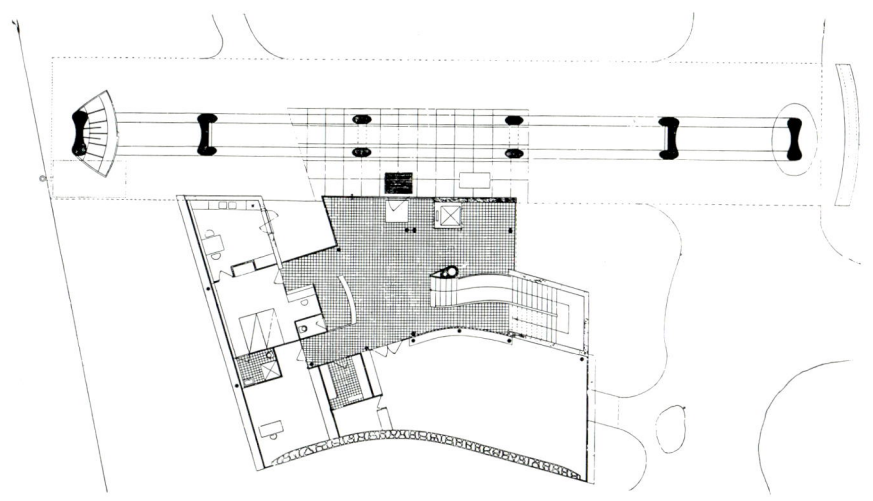

Lever House in New York, the UN building, Lucio Costa's famous Ministry of Health and Education in Rio de Janeiro, and many other office blocks or public buildings that have kicked out a flurry of subsidiary structures from the foot of the pure prism of a multi-storey slab. Corb's triumph, and the reason for his influence in this one work, was to have evolved a basic architectural solution that was patently rational, yet left room for a great deal of personal freedom: a slab of logic raised on a base of free invention.

Facing page: top: underneath the main block.

General Motors Technical and Research Centre, Warren, Michigan
Eero Saarinen and associates

It is obviously to the credit of a modern building that it shall appear to be exactly the concept that the hour requires—nothing could be more modern than that, and few buildings have achieved this more exactly than General Motors Technical Centre, the brain-box of the largest industrial enterprise the world has ever seen. Precise, mechanistic and repetitive in the 'endless' manner that fascinated the writers of the early fifties, it appeared to be the most perfect possible statement of a machine aesthetic for a repetitively mass-producing machine function. In conceiving it, Saarinen had contrived to isolate two basic ingredients of the architecture of Mies van der Rohe: the repetition of the parts, the classical formality of the whole. At GM, the repetiousness was emphasised by running it for immense distances along façades that were never resolved into symmetrical wholes, while the classical formality of symmetrical composition was reserved for a few selected end-walls, such as those of the test-houses, that were short enough to be be comprehended in a single glance. If a great master were to be vulgarised, this kind of radical intuition was clearly to be preferred to superficial plagiarism, and

The career and reputation of Eero Saarinen (1910–1961) have become increasingly enigmatic in retrospect. He did not emerge from the aegis of his famous father, Eliel Saarinen, until he designed the General Motors buildings at the beginning of the fifties, after which his rise was as meteoric as his output was bewilderingly varied. Cut off in mid-career, he begins to look like a congenital experimentalist who had not found a personal idiom, and maybe was never going to.

Facing page: GM Technical Centre, end wall of test-house.

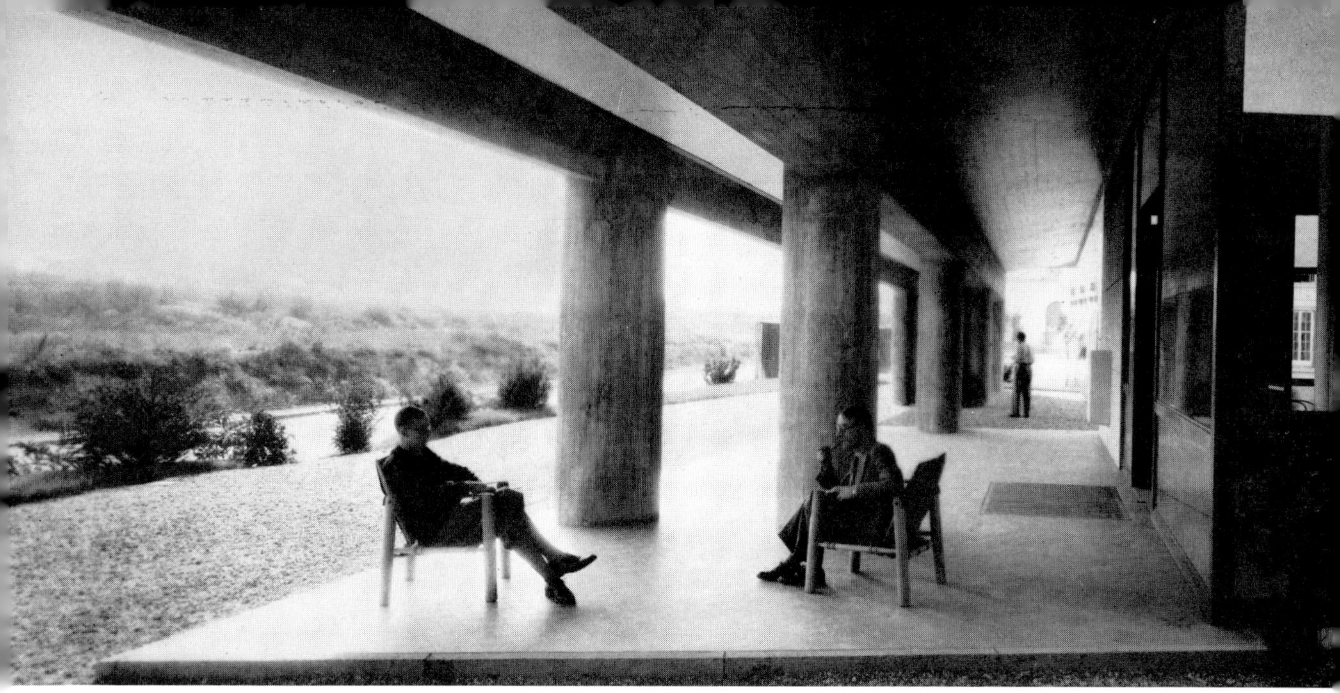

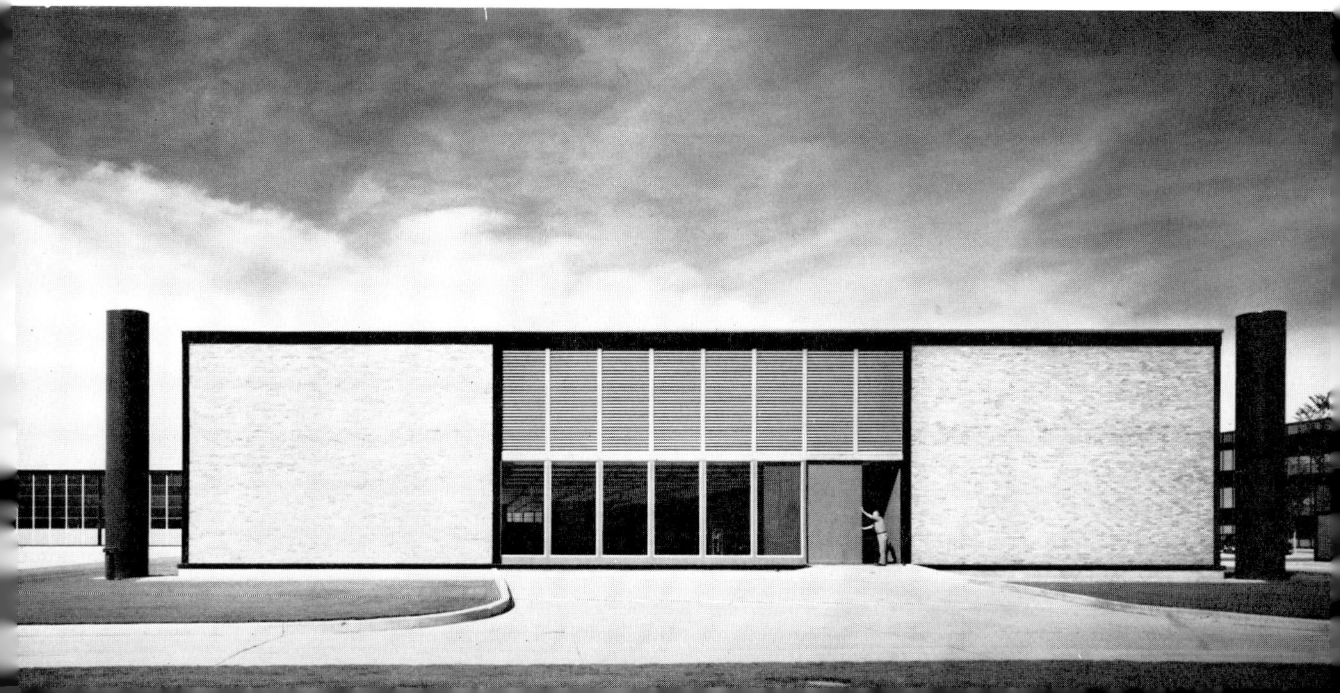

if non-rectilinear elements were to be permitted to invade the purity of the geometry, then it was clearly preferable that they should not be sloppy and free-form but, as here, taut and regular forms like those of the dome in the styling section, or the superb spheroid of the three-legged water tower. In addition, the whole complex was laid out with careful landscaping and on the most grandiose scale—an automotive Versailles, it was said—and meaningful contrasts were promptly drawn between the 'true' machine aesthetic of the buildings and the 'vulgar and deceptive' styling of the automobiles conceived inside them.

Such a card-house of unstinted and often unthinking adulation was bound to collapse under its own weight as soon as the hour that needed the building had passed, but Saarinen spectacularly beat the fan-club to it, and shot off at a tangent that superficially had more to do with the cars than with the buildings—in the Kresge auditorium (a dome) for the Massachusetts Institute of Technology, in the ice-hockey rink (a concrete-backboned permanent tent) at Yale, and the TWA terminal (a complex of complicated vaults) at Idlewild, he produced an architecture as curvaceous, and almost as acceptable to popular tastes, as Harley Earl's least inhibited General Motors car-styling. For a long time architectural opinion seemed stunned by this development; instead of being able to abuse GM Technical Centre as old-fashioned, they were too busy criticising its architect for being too new-fangled, and began to speak of GM as the last good building he designed. Now that he is dead, soberer counsels have prevailed, and the later works are beginning to be seen in perspective; the prim, trim rectangles at Warren are beginning to recover their rightful place as the *first* really good building he designed. It is, probably, the most consistently distinguished group of buildings ever designed for a major industrial concern, and it remains, in many ways, a model of one kind of architecture of technology, in its definition of a small structural unit within a larger concept of repetition, in the

Facing page: top: water tower and lake.
Bottom: styling building and domed auditorium.

115

definition of the relationship between panel and joint, and in its elaboration of the technical attributes of a pure rectangular aesthetic, all summed up, in one way and another, in the deep truss ceilings throughout the building which are, at the same time, part of the structure that holds it all up, and a very convenient place in which to stow a miscellany of piped and wired services to the rooms above and below. The technique itself was not invented by Saarinen, but he made better architecture out of it than anyone else had done before.

Airport Buildings, Gatwick
Yorke, Rosenberg and Mardall

The architecture of Gatwick airport has been talked up almost to masterpiece status; it has also been decried for the alleged dishonesty of wrapping a steel and glass curtain wall around a concrete-framed structure. Whatever the verdict, the mixture of materials must play a large part in it. Apparently uninfluenced by any dogma about this or that mode of construction, the architects have used any materials that came readily to hand for any particular section of the work. Below stairs (by road or rail, one enters two floors up) where the chunky concrete chassis is apparent, the material is taken at its face value (which is also its guts value) as a massive sub-structure to the passenger hall above. Internally, the concrete penetrates through the passenger hall as slim columns (paired where necessary) that rise clear and unashamed from the floor, until they meet the ceiling, which is a built-up plane of suspended panels. No two materials could be more different: the concrete prepared by traditional mud-and-water techniques on the site, the ceiling built up of dry, factory-produced components, yet they meet without embarrassment, and lie side by side as comfortably as the proverbial lion and lamb. No doubt this is to be attributed to the fact that both were selected by the same pair of minds (the junior partners, David Alford and Brian Henderson) as part of the same unified concept, which extends through the curtain walling (glass and black steel) also to the long finger (or 'jet-jetty') that takes the passengers out via an enclosed bridge structure to aircraft waiting on the apron.

Once this unembarrassed exploitation of the rich repertoire of modern materials has been seen and understood (not just condemned from dogma) two additional benefits are seen to accrue

Gatwick Airport, passenger hall.

from it. Firstly, the massive concrete unites the passenger buildings visually to the surrounding engineering works (by Sir F. Snow and Partners) with which they are, in any case, united functionally, such as the road ramps and footbridges over the railway. Secondly, for all that it is phrased in an idiom (based on Mies van der Rohe) that is supposed to be foreign, the building's refusal to be dogmatic about the use of materials gives it a sense of ease, of being at home, that is far more English than the forced, red-brick Anglicism of London airport. Well-engineered compromise—what could be more reassuringly English to the arriving traveller from abroad?

Facing page: top: air view of Gatwick, showing railway station, main building with finger, and through road with fly-overs leading to airport.

The Climatron, St Louis, Missouri
Murphy and Mackey

The fame of Buckminster Fuller is a phenomenon of the fifties when—the right man at the right time—he came suddenly to the forefront as Mister Number-One Space-Age-Designer. The acclaim was as justly earned as it was superficially given: given because his dome-shaped structures and their supporting non-rectangular mathematics caught the fancy of a generation that was bored with square architecture and ready for curves; Fuller's or Ronchamp's made no difference. But Fuller's emergence in the space decade was also just, because he considered the problems of human shelter in terms as rigorous as those forced upon the designer of a space capsule, and had been considering it in those terms for something like thirty years. The geodesic (great circle) domes were only one arm of his assault upon these problems, and it is a sad sick comment on the way we humans run our environment that fully-engineered versions of these domes have only been employed to provide fit habitations for radar installations, pigs and rare plants.

Yet the Climatron at St Louis is a fair representation of his

Buckminster Fuller's life and works contain sufficient incident, surprise and change of scene to make a film epic inevitable. Born in 1895 he had a conventionally disorderly college career, served in the US Navy and became interested in problems of human environment in the mid-twenties. Since then he has been free-booting on the frontiers of architecture, preaching a radical and scientific attitude to building design that architects find simultaneously fascinating and repellent. Official recognition did not really come until his domes for the US Marines in the early fifties, since when he has been one of the USA's leading cultural exports.

Facing page: bottom: the Climatron

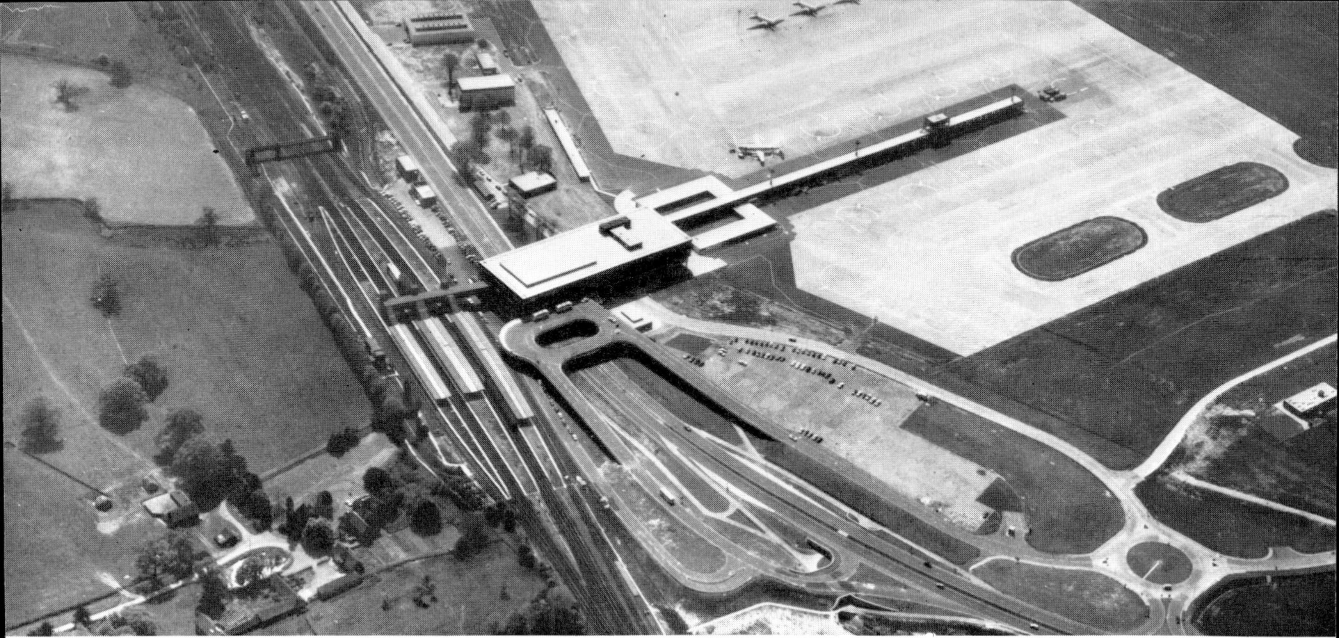

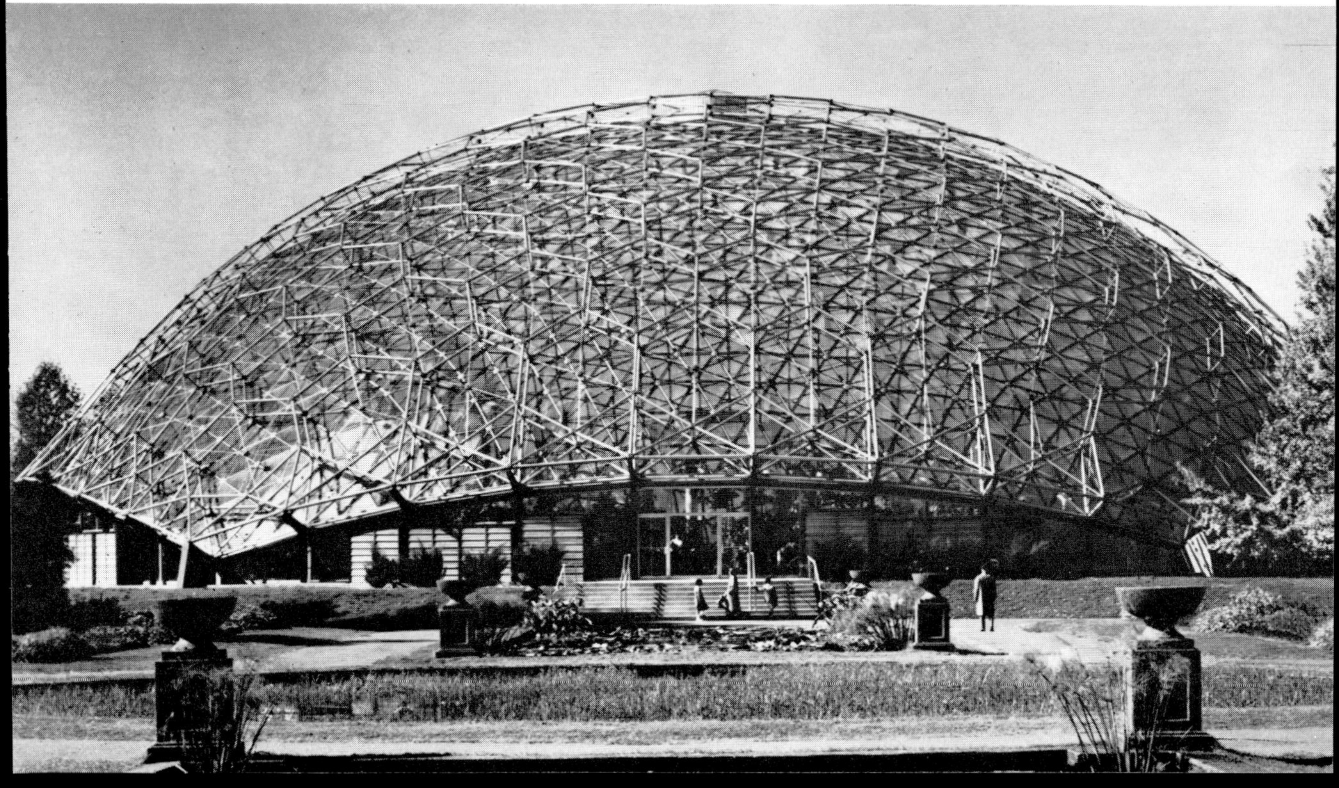

aims and ideas, working, as is usually the case, through the minds of other men who have licensed patents from him. A space-age greenhouse as surely as the Crystal Palace was a steam-age greenhouse, the Climatron is a spidery lattice dome full of carefully controlled climate, designed by the St Louis architects Murphy and Mackey (and it won them a major architectural prize). Fuller himself is on record with visions of gigantic domes soaring over garden environments which they shelter from the hostile climate outside, but the Climatron goes one better than this and maintains twelve *different* micro-climates to suit different sorts of plant ecology, requiring different admixtures of heat and humidity.

It achieves this result without any internal partitions, but simply through controlled flows of cooling or warming air, plus controlled local as well as general supplies of water. More, it does this without excluding the full natural sunlight through the transparent plastic that covers the dome, though at the cost of a fuel consumption that the ordinary greenhouse operator could not contemplate, and a battery of electronic aids that he could not afford. There are those who admit that the Climatron is a sort of earthly paradise, but deny that it is architecture, merely gadgetry. One can reply, on Fuller's behalf, that permanent structures are only one of the means by which an architect creates human environments today: electronics and other 'non-architectural' studies are further means to extend our control over environments, and if architects cannot make them part of their art then the human race may decide to disencumber itself of the art of architecture, just as it has disencumbered itself of the arts of witch doctors and professional rain-makers. Modern architecture must make good its claim to have something to say to a machine age.

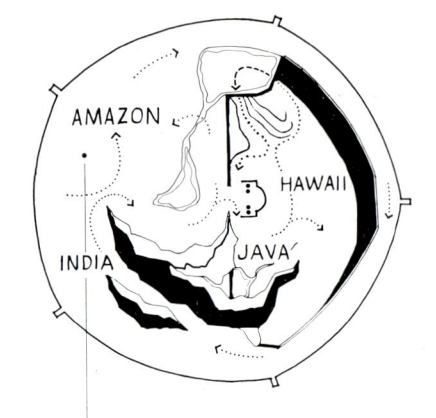

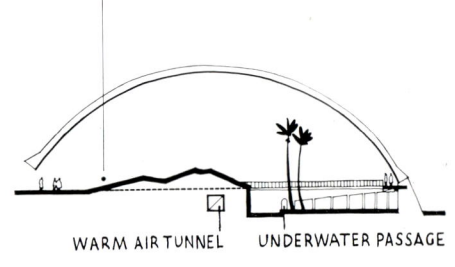

Plan and section of the Climatron. Facing page: interior.

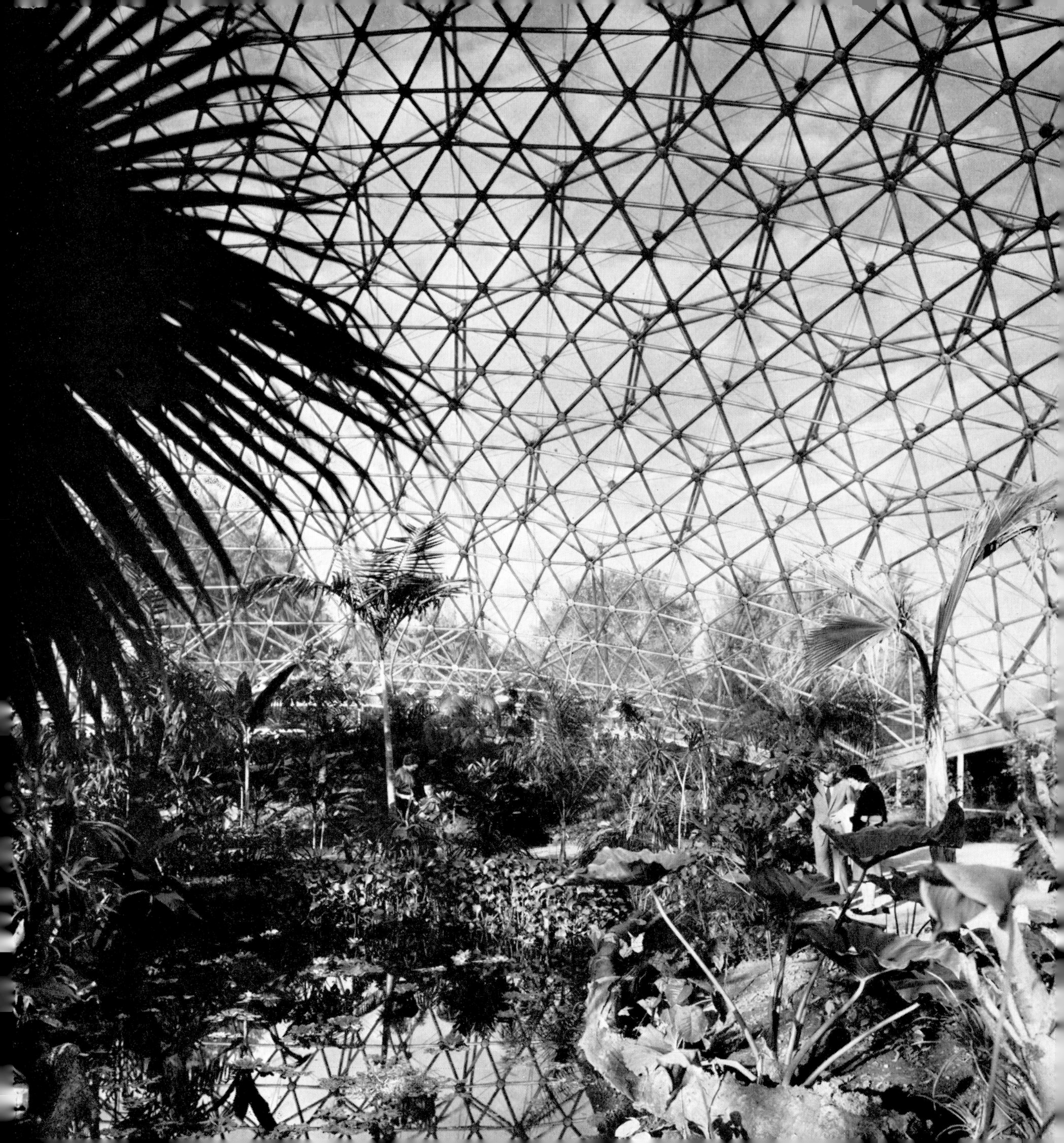

Harumi Apartment Block, Tokyo

Kunio Maekawa

Brutalism, as a going philosophy of architecture, has more aspects (sociology, town-planning, for instance) than the single one that has caught the public fancy, namely, the use of unfinished materials 'as found'. For some reason that the wise men of architecture have not yet elucidated, all aspects of brutalism seem uncommonly likely to occur in Japan. If ever a building was superficially Brutalist and Brutalist in depth as well, it is the big apartment block at Harumi by Kunio Maekawa; its publication in 1959 really startled the world. Superficially it is Maekawa's manifest pleasure in handling large lumps of stuff that makes it Brutalist —the great splay-footed concrete piers that hold it all up, the shameless great industrial water-tank on the roof, the cryptic numerals *15* in figures about six feet high on the end wall, the massive balcony fronts. Maekawa had passed through Le Corbusier's office briefly, and all these usages are Corb-inspired divergences from canonical Corbusian usages, such as one finds in the work of others regarded as Brutalists.

Yet more to the Brutal point is the bold, not to say blatant way in which the building expresses its structure and its operation: every fourth floor is simply a giant box beam, partly for structural reasons, partly to house duct-works and communications. This external rhetorical drama of the building as an operating mechanism is complemented by an extraordinary tenderness for the living habits of the tenants; each flat is effectively a traditional Japanese dwelling—*tokonoma*, mat-module-planning and all—slotted into place in the giant pigeon-hole system of the structure at large. Again, there is the attempt to make the building a unique and identifiable place, dear to all the Brutalist connection, and vindicated here by the local teddy-boys adopting its corridors and stairs for a suitable venue for their nocturnal rumbles. When

End view of Harumi block. Facing page: side view with water tank.

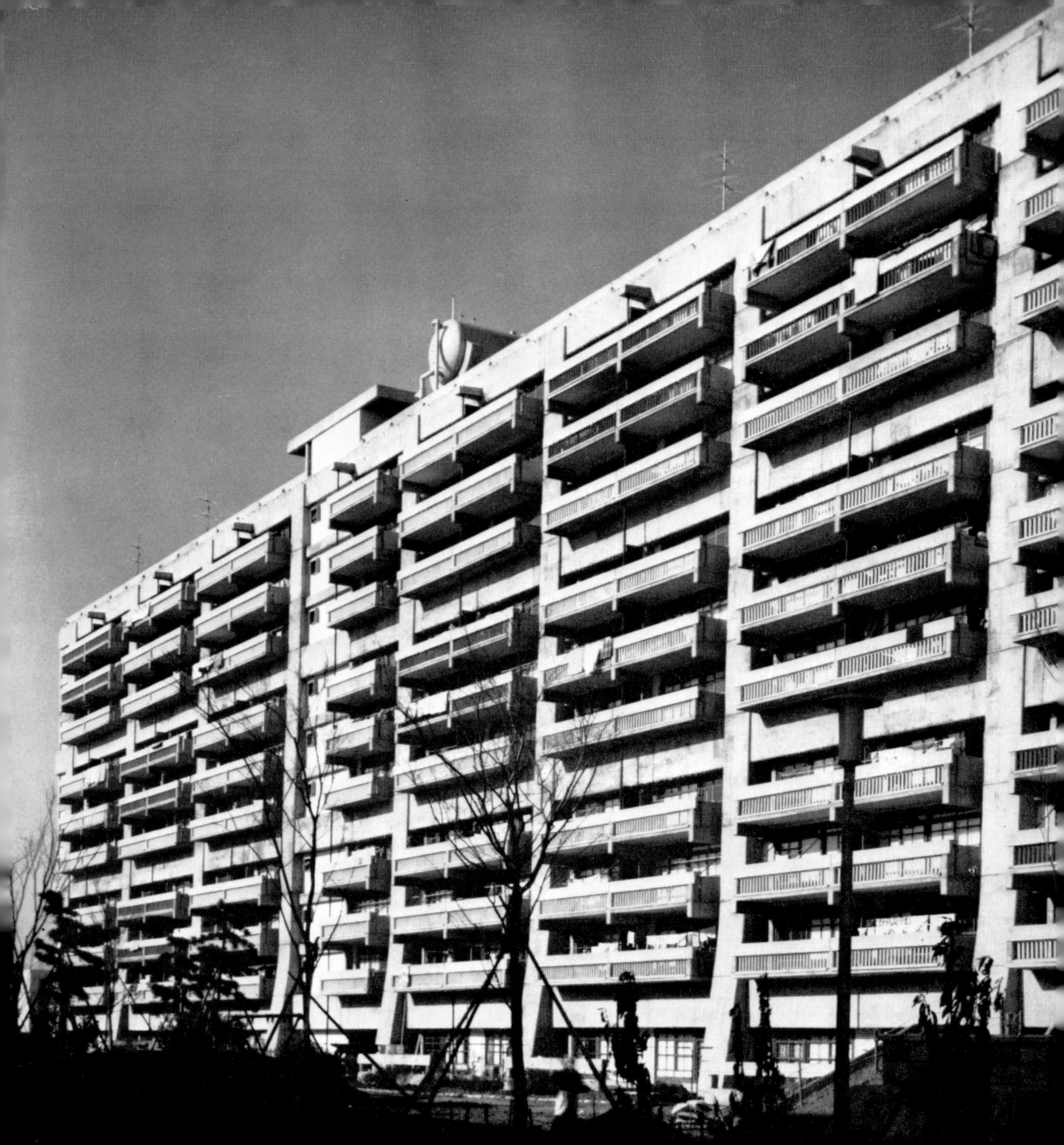

people rally to a place on purpose (even if the purpose is illicit combat) you know it has established itself, and the designer must be an architect who approaches people in a specially empathetic way. Social empathy is a mood that holds together much progressive architecture today—on this accounting, Park Hill in Sheffield, so different from Harumi in detail and in bulk, reveals itself as a close cousin of Maekawa's block. The mixture of heroic scale and domesticity, exposed mechanics and permissive sociability, are present in both. The mental infrastructure of modern architecture is international even where the forms are uniquely local.

Kunio Maekawa is a new name in world architecture, but he is no stripling, either in competence or in age—he was born in 1905. He studied in Europe in the thirties, including some time in the office of Le Corbusier as early as 1929-30, and counts as one of Japan's senior modernists.

Church at Imatra, Finland
Alvar Aalto

Too many of us respond to the mention of Scandinavian architecture with a stereotyped mental image of exquisite craftsmanship in teak and brick, harnessed to a conception of architecture so middle-of-the-road as to be entirely characterless. Yet, in all honesty, we know that the Baltic nations abound in architects of tremendous character, natural extremists: Jörn Utzon who conceived the sail-boat vaults of Sydney Opera House; Ralph Erskine of the 'underground' shopping centre at Lulea in the Arctic; Arne Jacobsen, most pure and extreme of European machine-aesthetes, as witness his town hall at Rodovre.

And Alvar Aalto—the Finn on whom superlatives fall as

Rodovre town hall.

Vuoksenniska church.

naturally and as plentifully as Arctic snow: giant, genius, form-giver, master-builder, wizard of the northern forests, and every word of it deserved. For thirty years, Aalto has been the quiet man of the Big Four; his name does not spring to mind quite as rapidly as those of Mies, Le Corbusier or Gropius, because his work is harder to classify and does not lend itself quite so readily to the accepted public-relations techniques by which architectural reputations are maintained. But Aalto is always there, and his buildings, unmistakably of our time but never entangled with our fashions, command a respect that is unlike that afforded to the work of the other masters.

There is, about most of his buildings, an unobvious, devious, obtuse and almost grudging charm that gives nothing away at first sight—Aalto can be a bit like that himself—but yields more and more to whoever is prepared to work away at it. His Vuoksenniska church at Imatra seems, at first look, to turn from the viewer and hide, humping its copper roofs defensively against the sky and lifting cautious windows, like watchful alligator eyes, above the white substructure in which it seems to burrow. This unyielding exterior has much to hide, since the interior volumes do not tally with the exterior bulk, though both express a plan and section that gives a narrow high apse at one end, and a broad flat tail at the other, where the entrance is. Each of the alligator eyes corresponds to a hump in the internal ceiling (not reflected in the roof-forms) over one of the three separate divisions of the interior.

What makes these divisions separate is a couple of sets of sliding partitions that can be rolled out of the walls of the processional porch by the tower. From the moment they begin to roll, everything is pure Aalto. They head straight across the nave, but in traversing the centre aisle each door passes through one of Aalto's favourite devices, a pair of coupled columns standing right in the aisle, and then the door curves round to follow the plan of the outer (but not the inner) window. Not only are the

A brilliant beginner, Alvar Aalto, made his first international impact with the Paimio sanatorium in 1930, when he was just thirty-two. He justified his world reputation with the memorable Finnish pavilions at the Paris Exhibition of 1937, and the New York World Fair of 1939. His status as a legend was confirmed when one of his finest early works, the library at Viipuri, was destroyed in the Russo-Finnish war, before the rest of the world had been able to get a proper look at it, and his later works have continued to reinforce the solid structure of his tremendous reputation.

Facing page, top: interior looking towards altar. Bottom: detail of vaults and sliding door-track.

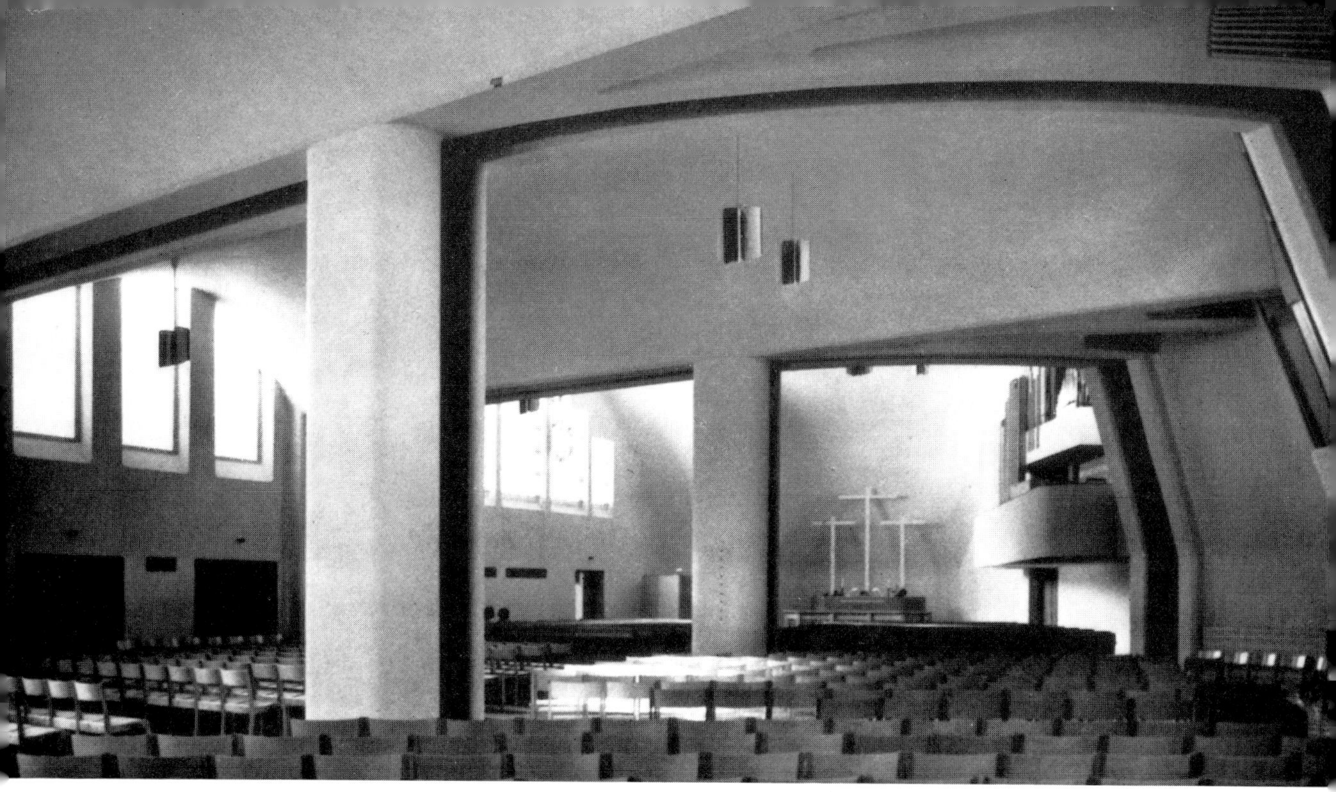

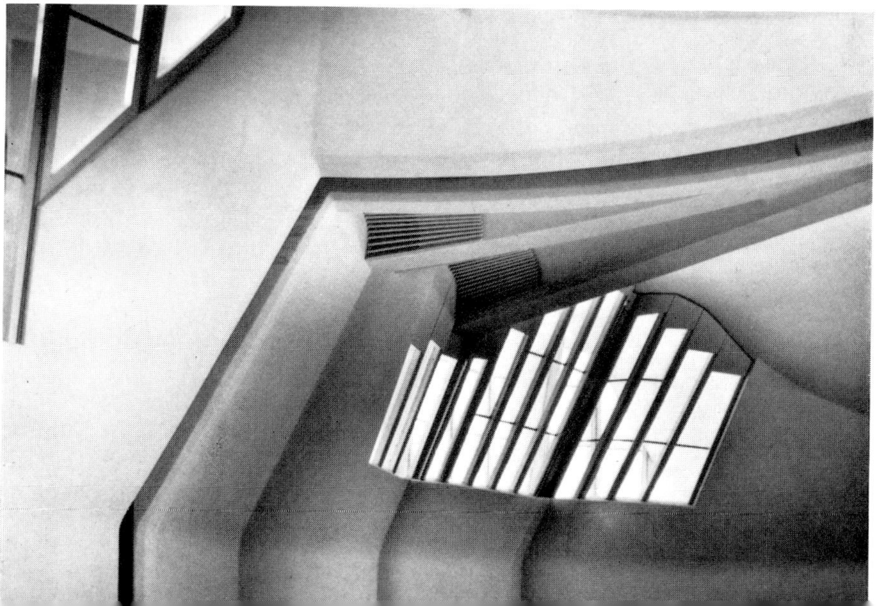

windows double, with the inner glazing sloping in to meet the humped ceiling, but the slightly arched structural beam that spans the nave beside the door tracks goes straight on when the door curves round. Absolute visual chaos seems inevitable, but Aalto avoids it, not by some radical simplification such as Corb might have introduced, but by piling on further complication: between the curving door-track and the straight beam he inserts two delicate, almost millinery, curved vaults with slatted ventilators in them.

It works—and the fact that it works is as Aalto as the blunt, non-communicative exterior; the effect as Finnish as the exquisite folk-paintings on the boarded ceilings of Finland's wooden country-Baroque churches. This too is part of Aalto's special genius: his ability to strike a resonance with folk traditions without ever copying them or being sentimental, without ever ceasing to be his own immensely sophisticated and hardheaded self.

Highpoint I and Highpoint II, Highgate, London
Lubetkin and Tecton

From the Penguin Pool onwards, the contribution of the Tecton partnership was a major part of the total momentum of the modern movement in England. Down to the Hallfield development in Paddington, every building was a battle won, and they remain as numinous as the monuments of heroes—none more so than the Highpoint complex in Highgate. With Highpoint 1, British modern architecture became man-size and internationally visible, and Le Corbusier set the seal of his approval on it by dubbing it the first 'vertical garden city'. By the standards of modern architecture it was an unconventional block, a doubled cross in plan, and its windows were far from gigantic or wallsize, but on the ends of the arms of the cross they were graced

Facing page: Highpoint 1.

1

by little balconies whose scrolled fronts scream 'thirties' even while they pass muster, still, as a convincing solution to the problem of finishing-off a particular kind of façade. Where the block is most convincingly modern-movement, however, is in the bold and plastic treatment of the entrance hall that runs most of the depth of the ground floor, and demands comparison with the first stirrings of modern (equally Corb-inspired) architecture in Brazil. The Corbusian inspiration need cause no surprise: his ideas went everywhere through the agency of intelligent men, like Lubetkin, in revolt against their academic training. His professionalism and bred-in-the-bone classicism, his rationalism and his rhetoric caught them where they lived and their own work took fire from it. In the entrance hall of Highpoint I the British saw for the first time that modern architecture could be a full-blooded visual art, as well as a conscience and a social programme.

All this was too much for the slow-witted citizens of Highgate, and when the Highpoint organisation wanted to develop the site next door (to prevent its misdevelopment by someone else) they found that the powers of aesthetic control that had lately been vested in local authorities as a defence against bad architecture could be used to prevent any kind of architecture at all. There ensured a comedy of desperate manoeuvres worthy of Ben Jonson, in which the local 'planners' were patiently flannelled into accepting, one by one, all the features of the new building, under the impression that quite different matters were under dispute. The outcome was not, perhaps, the best conceivable building for the site, but it is a worthy consort for Highpoint I, and its double-height living rooms were the right sort of next step forward.

But Highpoint II also has a front porch that has taxed the patience of the friends of modern architecture almost as much as Highpoint I taxed the minds of the Highgate villagers. The form, structure, applied lettering and practically everything else

Facing page: top: hall of Highpoint I, bottom: porch of Highpoint II.

HIGHPOINT

about that porch are as resolutely modern as anyone could have wished in the thirties, but where there ought to be slender steel columns to hold it up, there are—of all things—casts of one of the Erechtheum caryatids, from the British Museum. It was (and is) completely indefensible, but it clearly comes from the same classics-based professionalism as gave us the rest of the scheme, and the architects have defended it with the same forensic brilliance as they used to make rings round the villagers' aesthetic objections to Highpoint I. Now that the increasing sophistication of us all has made Lubetkin's classicism more obvious and his modernism less so, this Hellenic pin-up seems less of an affront to progress than it once did; no more than a classicist's sign-manual . . . until you think of the fantastic self-confidence needed to do it at a time when your strongest supporters had only just cured themselves of regarding Greece as the be all and and end all of artistic excellence. . . .

Park Hill, Sheffield
City Architect, J. L. Womersley

Ever since the war we have had the curious spectacle in Britain of social programmes that were grandiose in scale, being realised in penny packets of architecture. Very good packets, at their best, like the isolated towers of the L C C's Roehampton development, scattered through the established greenery of their beautiful site like off-white Monet girls in an impressionist garden. But where, demanded a generation regarding with despair the coy scale of the New Towns, where is the building that is as big as the sociology?

Sheffield gave the answer, but not until the beginning of the sixties. On a straggling, sloping site at Park Hill, the City Architect's Department rehoused an entire slum clearance area in one gigantic building whose sheer size would be sensational anywhere

Roehampton blocks, from Richmond Park.

Park Hill from the air.

in the world (three times as much accommodation as the Unité at Marseilles) and yet the gross social statistic is less important than the concept of sociability that is the backbone of the whole design. The concept is made manifest by a system of broad street-decks that run like a literal backbone, right through the building, as it snakes and forks its precipitous way down the slope: a drop equivalent to nine storeys in height. The decks, that make it possible to get from one end of the building to any of its four other ends without going down to ground level, are big enough to admit tradesmen's pedestrian-controlled delivery-trucks and stray bicycles, but they are free from normal death-dealing types of wheeled traffic and, since the doors of all the apartments open on to one or another of the decks, they become the real backbone of social communication and grouping as well —at corners and other natural points of human aggregation, kids play, mums natter, teenagers smooch and squabble, dads hash over union affairs and the pools.

You can walk for ten minutes along one of these decks, as it threads its way first along one side of the block and then the other, alternating stunning panoramas of the city with close views into interior spaces partly walled in by the arms of the block. The architectural detail with which one is immediately surrounded is plain and blunt; not all of it will stand very intensive study in isolation, but when you stand back from the block at the down-hill end and peer up at the fourteen-storey cliff of habitation from the depths of the Sheaf Valley, the details dwindle into insignificance, even though the sense of human presence does not.

Opinions are divided, even so, about what happens to the human presence on this scale. Serious critics like Lewis Mumford believe the scale of the block to be inhumanly vast, others decry the social concept (which meant so much to the young architects who conceived it) as mere 'matiness'. Only time and research will show whether either objection is justified, but there can be no doubt that Sheffield has acquired a building and a townscape feature that is in a class by itself, realised in the teeth of a site that would have deterred lesser men than the boys of the project team responsible: Jack Lynn, Ivor Smith and Frederick Nicklin.

However, their true mastery of the design seems less powerfully manifest at the extremes of scale—the sheer size of the site, or the close domesticity of the decks—than in the middle range, where such designs so often go wrong. Park Hill reveals its

Everyday views of the street decks. Facing page: junction point, with lift and stair towers, and deck bridges.

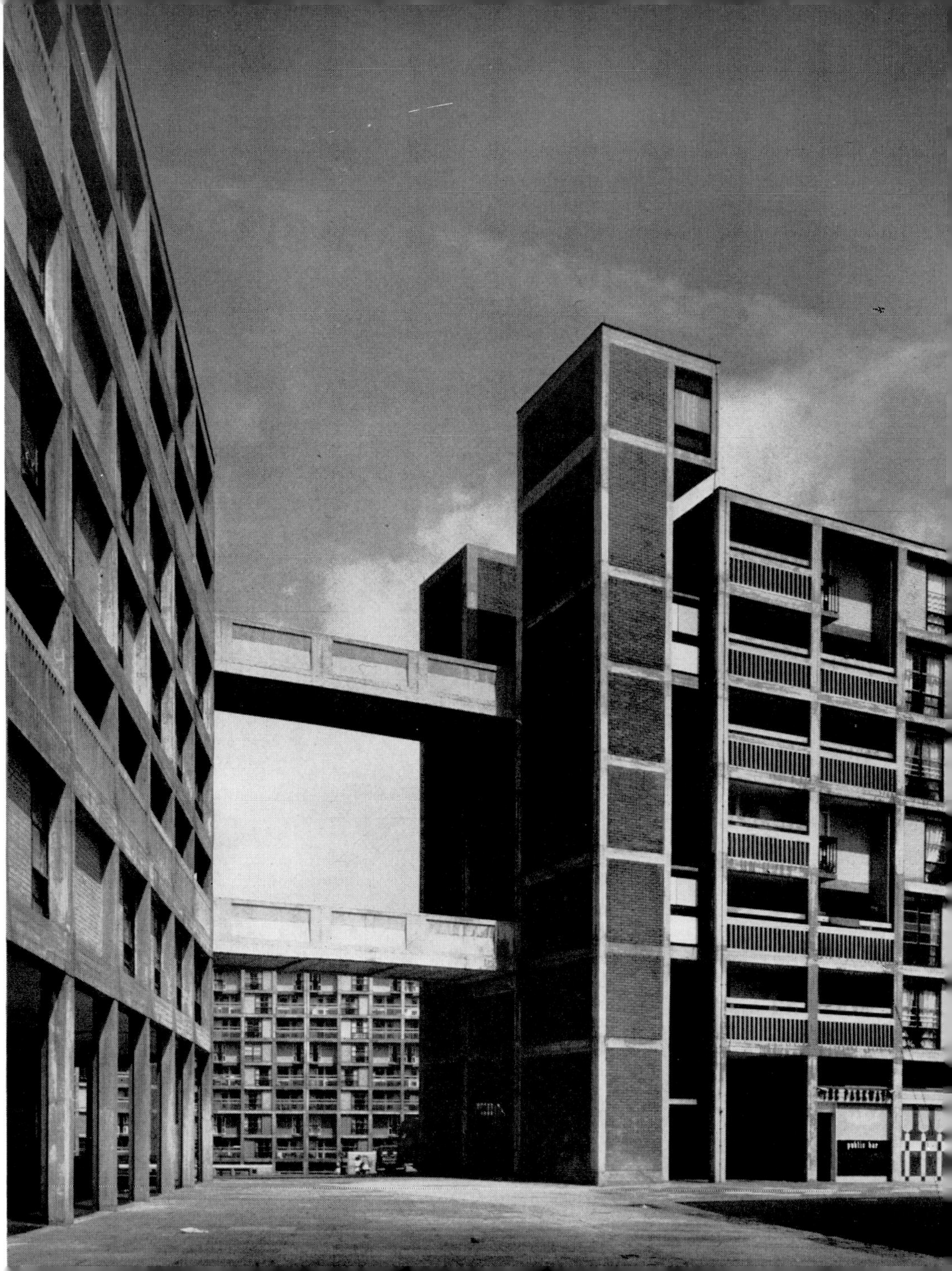
public bar

inmost secrets with the greatest architectural conviction at the three points where the block bifurcates, which are also the only three points where access roads are allowed to penetrate into the pedestrian-sacred precincts within. To accommodate these multiple functions, one limb of the block halts, with the customary pair of vertical circulation ducts (one for lifts, one for stairs) that happen wherever a block ends. But at this juncture, a horizontal circulation duct—a bridge carrying a street deck—leaps from the landing serving the lifts and stairs, across the access road to connect with the street deck at the same level on the two divergent limbs opposite. At these points, especially where as many as three deck-bridges are superimposed across a single gap, Park Hill states unequivocally that it is a gigantic structure held together by pedestrian circulation—that is, men, women and children, walking along, on the scale and at the pace of the human race.

Street-decks and pedestrian bridge at junction-point.

Brasilia, Brazil
Oscar Niemeyer, Lucio Costa and others

Chandigarh, East Punjab
Le Corbusier (architect for the Capitol)

Brasilia is the world's dream of an architect's dream—to create a new city on an unspoiled site; it's what architects dream of in novels. Better still, capital-city splendours were built into the contract from the beginning. Chandigarh falls short of this dream because much of the city had been laid out by other hands before Le Corbusier set foot on the site. He got the corner reserved for capital splendours, but not the city. Against this, Brasilia has complications of divided command: Oscar Niemeyer is the head man, and is designing the government buildings, but the city-plan is the work of Lucio Costa, who won the right to

Facing page: Plan of Brasilia. Key: 1. Government centre; 2. Ministries; 3. Cathedral; 4. Cultural centre; 5. Business and traffic centre; 6. Broadcasting centre; 7. Municipal centre; 8. High-density housing; 9. Low-density housing; 10. Sports area; 11. Railway Station; 12. Industrial area; 13. Airport; 14. Embassies; 15. University city; 16. Tourist hotel; 17. President's Palace.

137

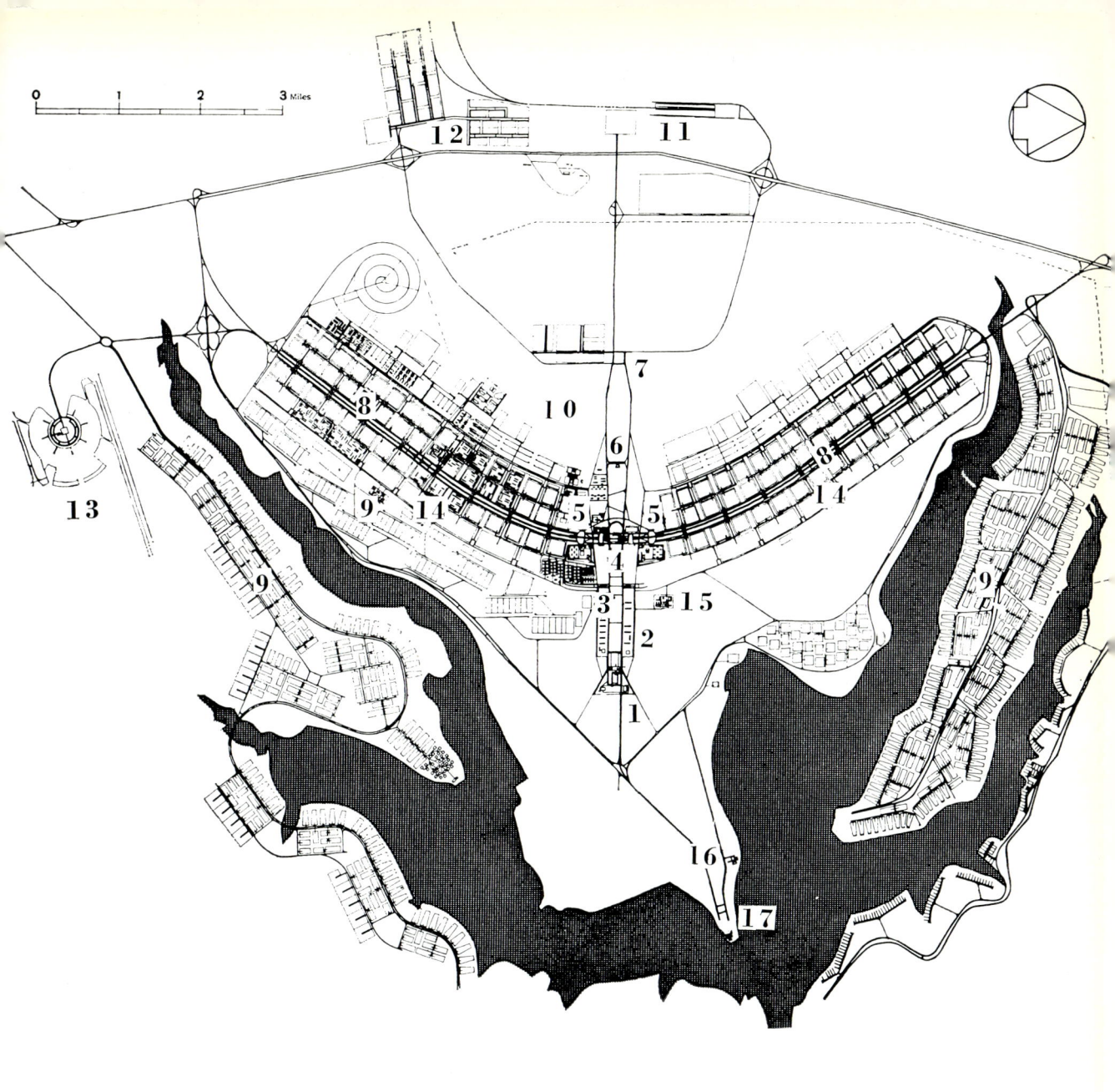

this most coveted of jobs in open competition. And Costa could hardly be Niemeyer's subordinate since he was his boss on the team that designed the celebrated Ministry of Health in Rio that launched the Brazilian school on its triumphant progress towards—Brasilia.

But, at least, the style in which both men are grounded is the same, was invented by them for the Ministry on the basis of some sketches by Le Corbusier who was briefly consultant on the project. In Brasilia that style of contrasting geometries, one square and regular, the other irregular and curved or angular, has been pushed to systematic extremes. It happens not only in the building themselves, but in the relations of building to building, even in the town-plan, where the hard straight line of the 'governmental axis' slashes through the vague free-hand curve that outlines the residential area. Along the roads, straight or curved, are ranged blocks that exhibit the contrasted geometries as a matter of course, plain and square in bulk form, but raised on fancy pilotis and crowned by free-form roof-structures. Ten years ago the accomplishment with which the Brazilians handled this style was the envy of the world, now it is as commonplace as the way the Americans use curtain walling. However, Niemeyer's use of the two geometries is no more commonplace than Mies van der Rohe's use of curtain walls.

In the Presidential palace, he has condensed the two geometries into a single rectangular box, its immensely spacious interior laid out with simple grandeur and without curved walls, while the second geometry appears, with tremendous effect, only in the leaping curves of the swan-like arcading that supports the loggias that shelter the palace walls all round. Against this, the Parliament building represents a more conventional reading of the Brazilian style, but pushed to its last extremity of elaboration. The single tall slab has twinned, and become equivocal: is it two slabs of office accommodation standing close together, or is it a single administrative block split down the middle? At all events,

It seems to be supposed that Niemeyer (born 1907) gets all the credit while Costa (born five years earlier) does all the work; or that Niemeyer has inspiration, while Costa has only application. Yet Costa won the right to lay out the town of Brasilia with a scheme whose overwhelming recommendation was that it took off from a stroke of inspired imagination. What seems more likely is that Costa, sheltering under the edge of his official appointments, is in a position to implement imaginative gestures on behalf of other people, such as calling in Le Corbusier as consultant on the Ministry of Education in Rio.

Facing page: Brasilia, top: President's Palace; bottom: Parliament building.

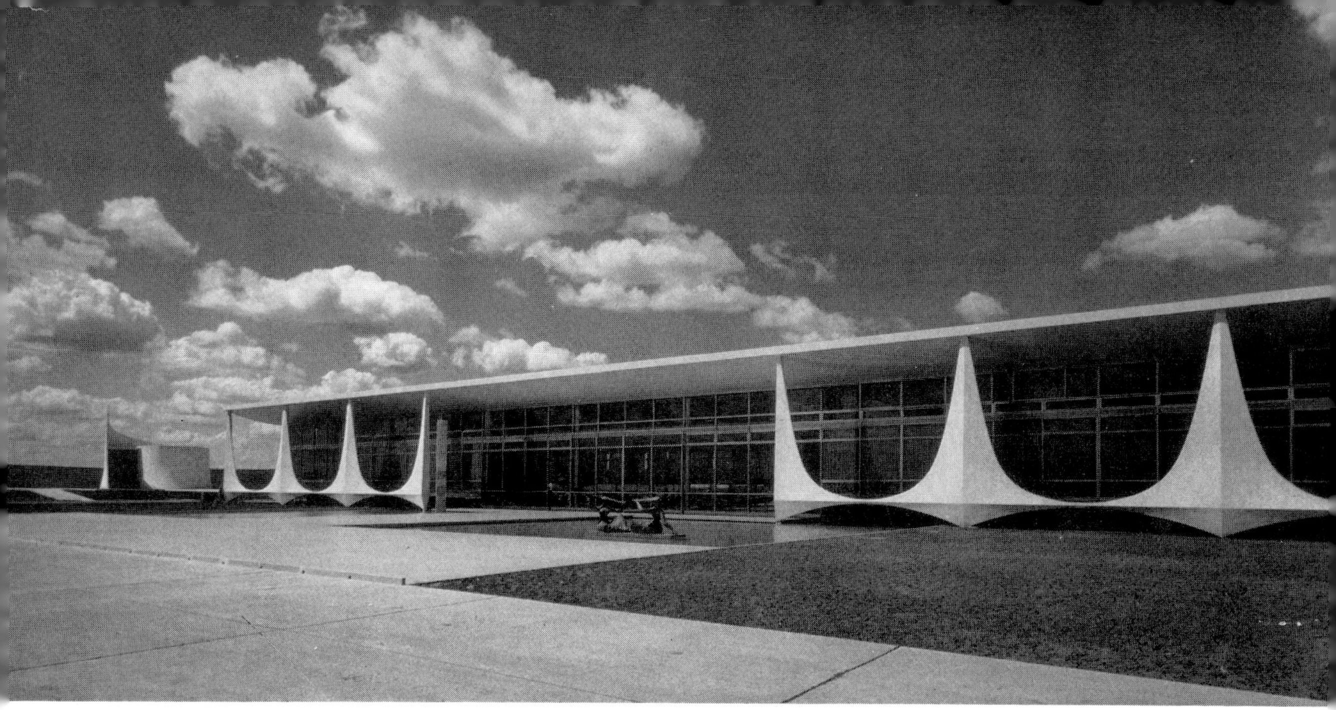

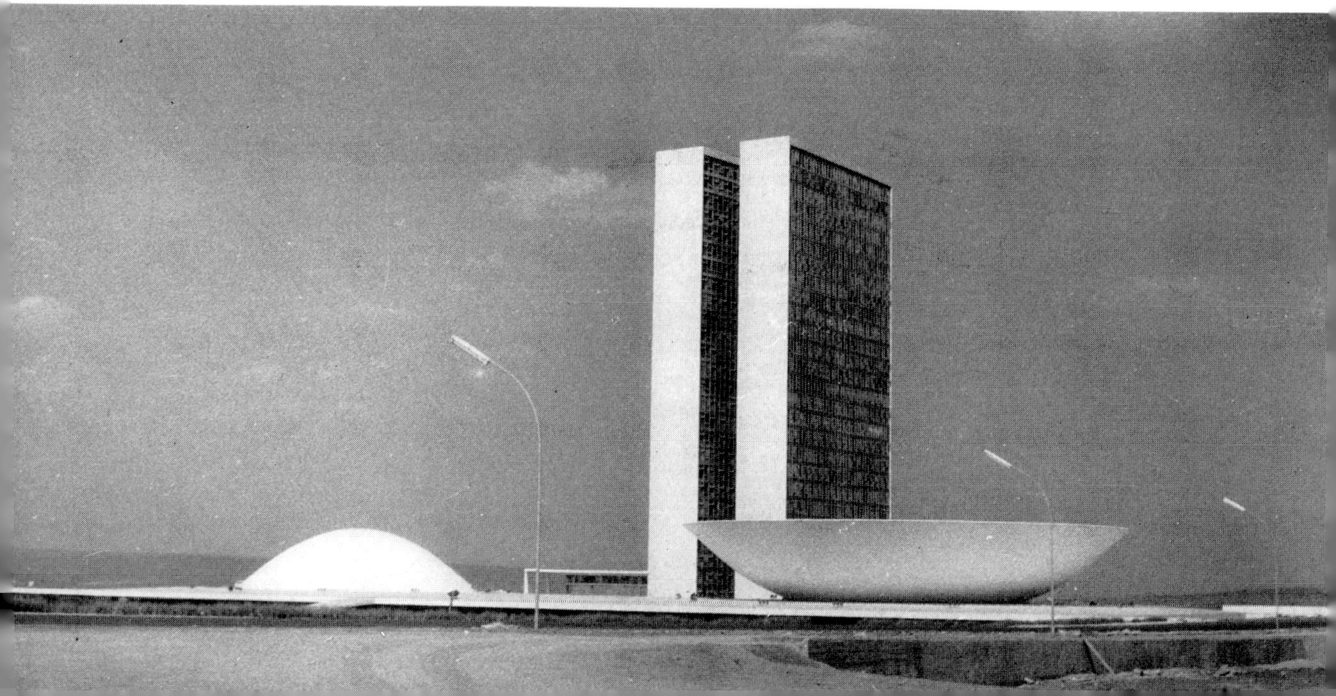

the old easy simplicity and clarity are gone, and replaced by a sophistication that makes earlier Brazilian architecture look naïve (which it often was, bless its progressive aspirations!). Under the twinned slab, and at right angles to it (as usage dictates) lies (as usage also dictates) a horizontal element terminating not in a single auditorium (as in the universal prototype, the Ministry of Health) but crowned by two council chambers, one in the form of a low dome, the other in the same form but the other way up; a saucer. But if both are chambers (one for senators, the other for deputies) how can they be truly functional and yet such different shapes? Both in practice are fairly loose fits on functions that, after all, are determined by human relationships, not mechanical operations, and the complementary forms are justifiable as architecture of a grand, rhetorical simplicity.

And, functional or not, they are still modern architecture as we have known it, clean, crisp, precise (and all that jazz), the product of the kind of sweeping self-confidence that is necessary to clear a slum or found a capital. Nothing could be more different than the government buildings at Chandigarh. There, it looks as if Corb had read that the late work of a great master is broad, rough, inscrutable and deceptively simple, and had decided to play it by the book. Comparisons between Chandigarh and late Beethoven quartets have already been voiced, further corn about Rembrandt and Michelangelo is to be expected. Yet the fact remains that the simplicities, almost crudities, of Le Corbusier's design for the Law Courts, with a row of justice-boxes simply shacked up under a concrete sunshade makes Niemeyer's most sophisticated work look brash; the jazzy breaks in the rhythm of the regular fenestration of the Chandigarh secretariat, caused by the intrusion of double-height ministerial rooms, make Costa's ritual separation of parts look jejune; and Le Corbusier's planning, conceived in terms of vast rectangles of earth pegged out with obelisks, makes Costa's

Another view of the Parliament building. Facing page: Chandigarh, top: Secretariat; bottom: Law Courts.

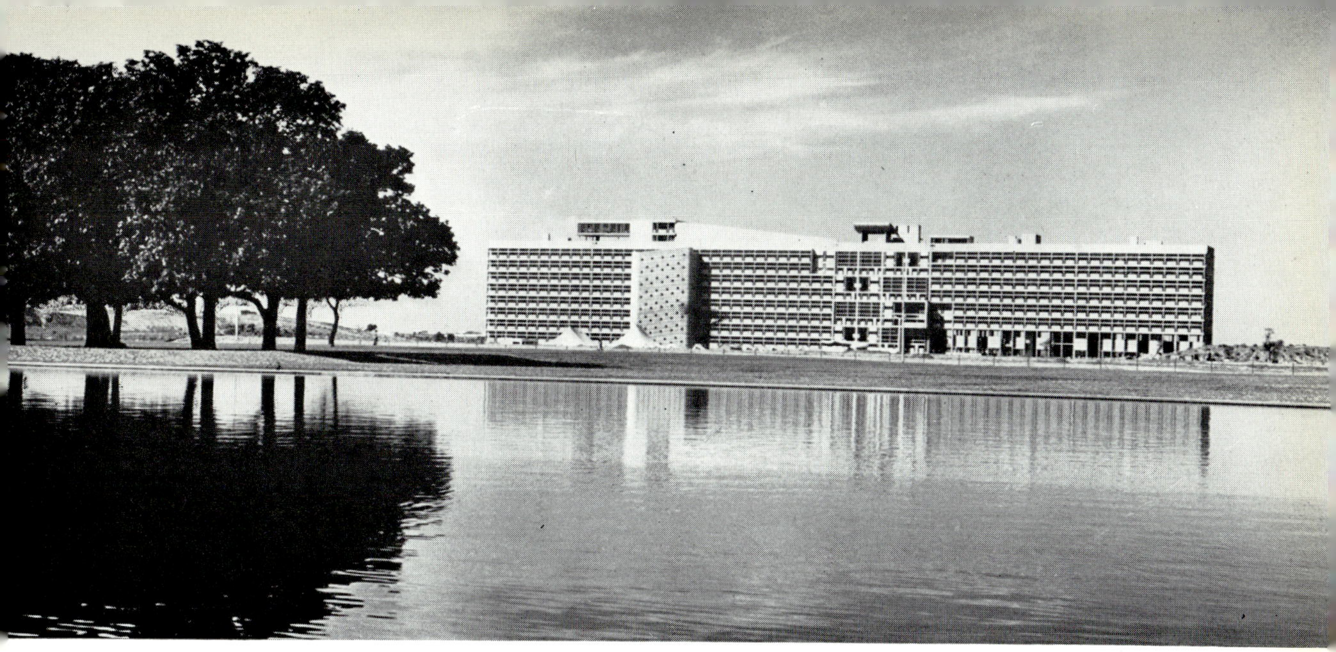

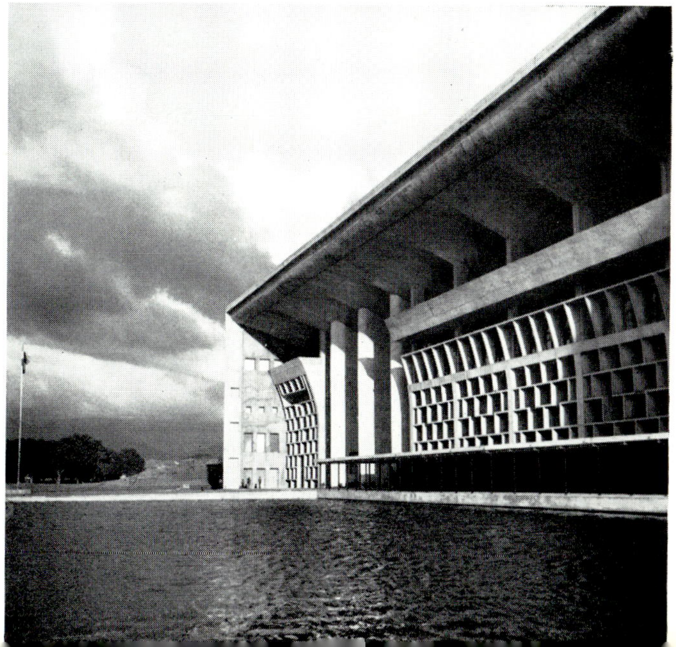

plan for Brasilia look only a little more subtle than borough surveyor's work.

Only, Costa is right and Corb wrong, as far as one can see. The conception of planning that groups the buildings of the Capitol at Chandigarh is very very old indeed; it belongs to the peasant-powered, peasant-paced world before machine technology; a world where mere horizontal extent was laboriously impressive to the pedestrian, and the mere presence of geometry was numinous proof of the triumph of the human will over natural chaos. A couple of successful Five Year Plans, or a flush of wheeled affluence in the Punjab, will make nonsense of this before the buildings have had a chance to acquire the air of hoary reverence that makes the piddling courts of the Louvre impressive even to those who normally live at turnpike scale. But Costa has planned Brasilia in terms that would be generous even on a community that had two Cadillacs in every garage. His module is circulation, and the highest drama of his town is where major traffic streams meet, fuse and resolve themselves again in his multi-level town-square. Compared with this, Corb's Chandigarh already begins to command the archaeological interest of the Acropolis.

Facing page, top: plan of Chandigarh. Key: 1. Le Corbusier's Capitol complex; 2. City centre; 3. University; 4. Industrial area; 5. Grain and timber markets; 6. Lake; 7. Town Park.

C.L.A.S.P. School, Milan
Nottingham County Architect's Department

Committees, group-practices and other forms of collective design are so often blamed for bad architecture that it has become the current cant that they can never produce any good architecture at all. I have been told that all Britain's post-war schools must be bad because they were designed by 'committees of civil servants'. Yet, on one of the rare occasions that a British, 'committee-designed' school was exposed to international competition, the international jury awarded it the biggest prize they had to offer, and then up-graded the prize because they felt it was not

Facing page: CLASP school, Milan.

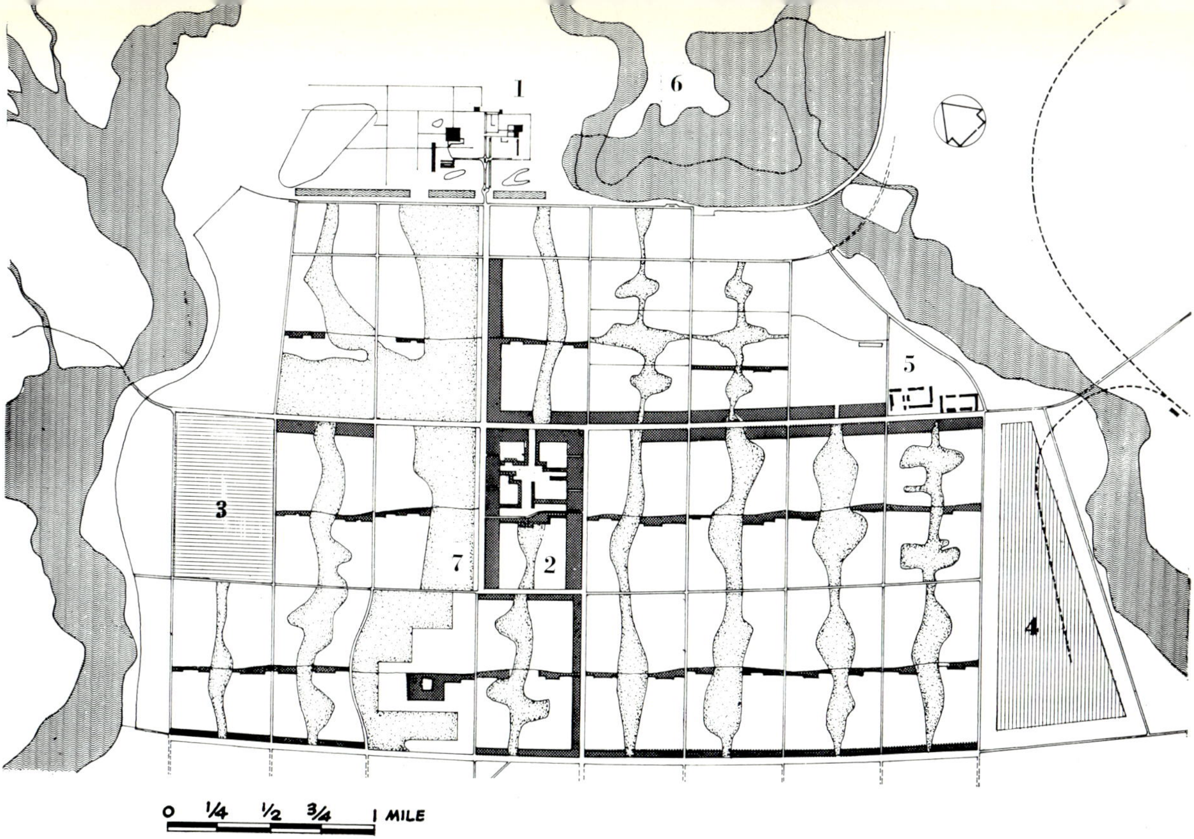
1
2
3
4
5
6
7
0 1/4 1/2 3/4 1 MILE

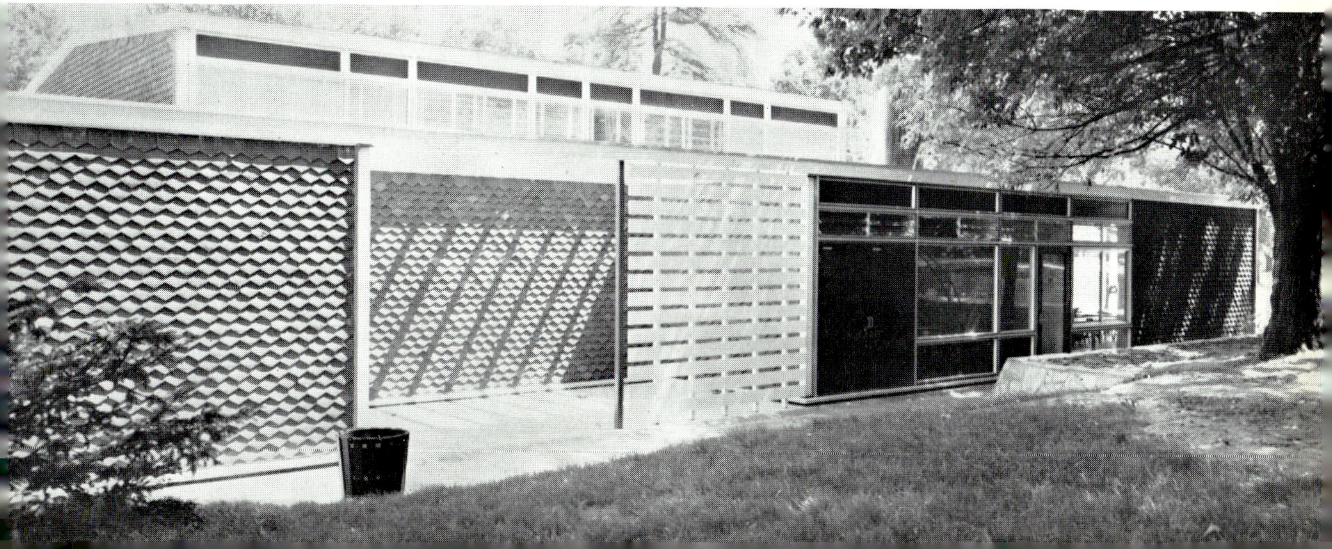

as big as the virtues it was meant to celebrate. That *Gran Premio con Menzione Speziale* at the 1960 Triennale (three-yearly exhibition of architecture and design) in Milan went squarely where it belonged—to the Nottinghamshire architect's department, and the CLASP system of construction—of which more anon.

The fact is, obviously, that there are bad groups and prize-class groups, and there are different kinds of good architecture. If architecture is only allowed to be good when it starts as a thundering statement of an individual personality, then not even a prize-class design-group can produce it. But if good architecture starts with a human need clearly understood and imaginatively served, then a group big enough to undertake research, before design, is able to provide good architecture. There is no magic about this: the group has to consist of real talents; it has to be organised to get the best out of them; and its relationship with the outside world must be good, too. In the newly established English tradition of 'development-group design' that relationship starts with research into the requirements of the users; in schools, into adapting the planning to the most advanced teaching methods.

But Nottingham is also a member of CLASP — the Consortium of Local Authorities Special Programme—which pools research and information on structures, cost-cutting, bulk-buying, etc., between a group of Local Authorities in the North Midlands. Out of the special requirements of these authorities (such as the consequences of mining subsidence) has come a constructional system, a kit of parts, that is now the CLASP thumb-print internationally, and was largely responsible for that *Gran Premio*.

Among prefabricating systems it is one of the world's weirdest —the pioneers of modern architecture saw prefabricating systems as ruthlessly logical, simple, cut to the minimum of components, and this view has become the ideal. But the CLASP system, which is real, not ideal, is only as logical as it needs to be, only simple enough to get by, and by no means minimal: it

Entrance front.

often offers more than one way of solving a problem, such as the cladding of a wall. The range of choice (almost unknown in other prefabricating systems) still gives the ratepayers better schools for less public expenditure, but it also gives quite a lot of architects a chance to get on and design a building that serves the needs of the user, without having to spend hours drawing out details. The user of CLASP has at his fingertips a set of ready-designed details that combine together naturally into architecture.

And that isn't magic either; a lot of mental sweat went into the first creation of the system to make sure this would happen, and a lot of continuing research has been needed to make sure it goes on happening as the system is developed further. In Milan, it worked beautifully, and world design leaders could see, for instance, how the framing of the window automatically tidied up the otherwise ragged edge of the tile-hanging. Maybe this was not architecture in Le Corbusier's classic definition of 'magnificent, cunning and correct play of masses brought together in light', but the Italian sunlight, which shows up most mistakes in architecture, could only show how cunning and correct CLASP was. If magnificence was missing, so was the pomposity that results from trying to be magnificent in the wrong context—and, in this context, most reasonable men would settle for CLASP.

Facing page, top: services unit.

The Bauhaus, Dessau
Walter Gropius

The present state of the Bauhaus is the enduring shame of the modern movement. Not that anyone can do much about it while Germany is halved and it lies beyond the Iron Curtain: decrepit, damaged, derisorily restored, its famous walls of glass reduced to small square windows, in a 'provisional' brick skin. But if it were possible to do anything to mend its ravaged face, there are many who would be glad to have it off their consciences.

Why be so concerned? For two reasons. Firstly it is a sacred site, where Walter Gropius gave architectural and institutional form to a concept of design education that has changed the world, and inspires, enrages, supports and depresses design-teachers even today, forty-five years after he first began to rough it out. The first Bauhaus, which he founded at Weimar in 1919 was already dedicated to the heart-and-hand concept of learning by doing, education through knowledge of materials and tools. At Dessau the concept could be extended to include the reasoning mind and machine production. The new buildings there had a machine-shop as well as studios, and the architecture school—as befitted the eagles' nest of a new age that Gropius savoured as sharply as the Futurists did—was on a bridge spanning a road

Facing page, bottom: the Bauhaus, workshop block on right.

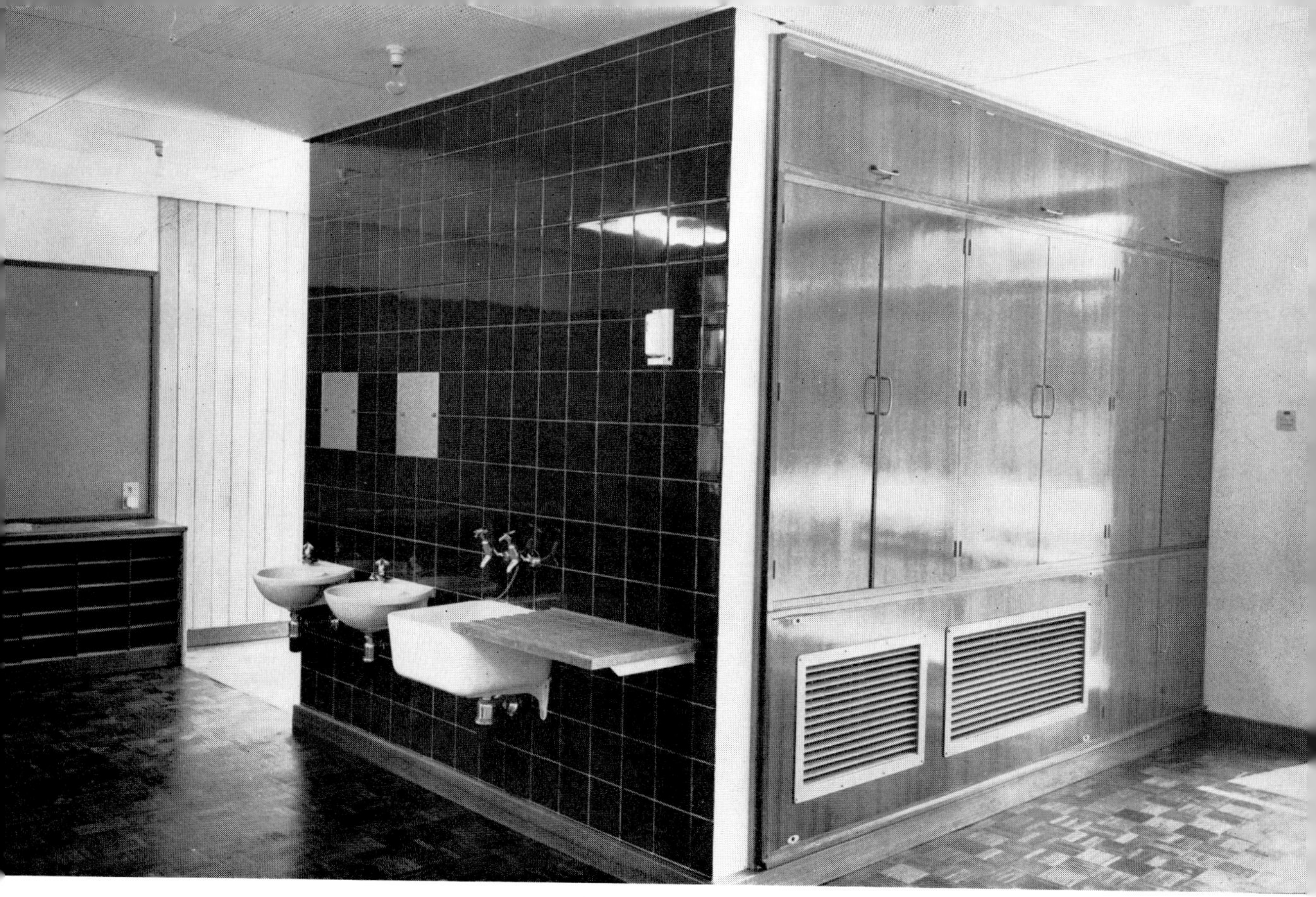

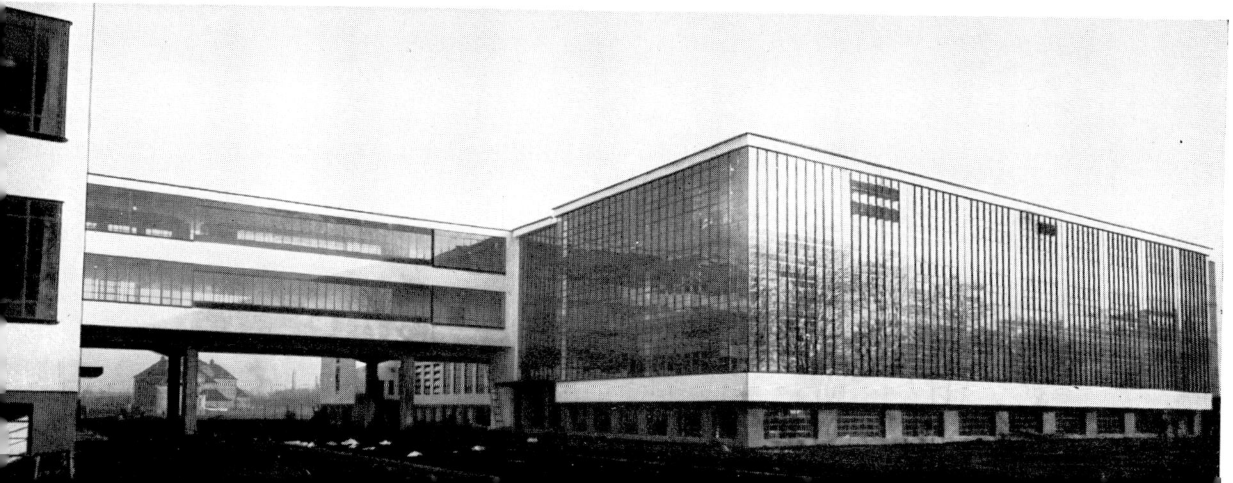

between two blocks. This was not an ingenious necessity inspired by a difficult site, for the ground had been wide-open and suburban when Gropius began to design; the relationship of building to road was of Gropius's own making, the road was there because he put it there. A manifesto building, then, for a motorised age.

Secondly, it was more than a manifesto, it was a masterpiece: the first really big masterpiece of the modern movement, the full powers of the new architecture deployed for the first time on a scale too big to be dismissed as mere domestic eccentricity. Gropius presented to the world a large, multi-purpose structure cast entirely in the new idiom, and so convincingly that there could no longer be any doubt that this idiom was an architecture in its own right, as surely as Gothic or Georgian. But the mastery exhibited by Gropius at this master moment of his career, goes deeper than the mere management of a style. The Bauhaus buildings at Dessau, in their original condition, were modern right the way through. The functional grouping of the parts may appear loose, with the building hooking out into the landscape in three right-angled arms, but there is no suggestion of the building falling apart visually. From all aspects—and it is meant to be seen from all sides—the separate elements are seen to group themselves satisfactorily in a manner that never fails to reveal the underlying formal order of the whole, the difference of construction and fenestration revealing the functional order that underlies the forms, and nowhere more powerfully than in the all-glazed wall, now no more, of the workshop block.

Sigfried Giedion has called it a space-time composition, revealing itself only to a moving observer as he circulates round it, but such an observer should also move *through* it, because as he passes under the celebrated bridge he will find himself at one point in the middle of a balanced symmetrical composition, with identical and equal entrances facing one another on opposite sides of the road, serving identical stairs lit by identical windows.

Walter Gropius's long career—he was born in 1883—will be one of the most splendid and baffling in modern architecture when the historians come to try and sum it up. Few men have done so much to create the mental and moral atmosphere that made modern design possible, few have tried so hard to conceal their lights under bushels of anonymity —nor failed so often escape public notice. By disposition a grey eminence and inspirer of others, as in his ten years of teaching at the Bauhaus and twenty at Harvard, he has been constantly forced to the front of the stage by the pressure of events, and now seems likely to finish his career in the full glare of the spotlights as one of the architects of the world's largest and most controversial office block, the Pan-Am building at Grand Central Station in New York.

Facing page: top: another view, below: plan at first floor level.

BAUHAUS

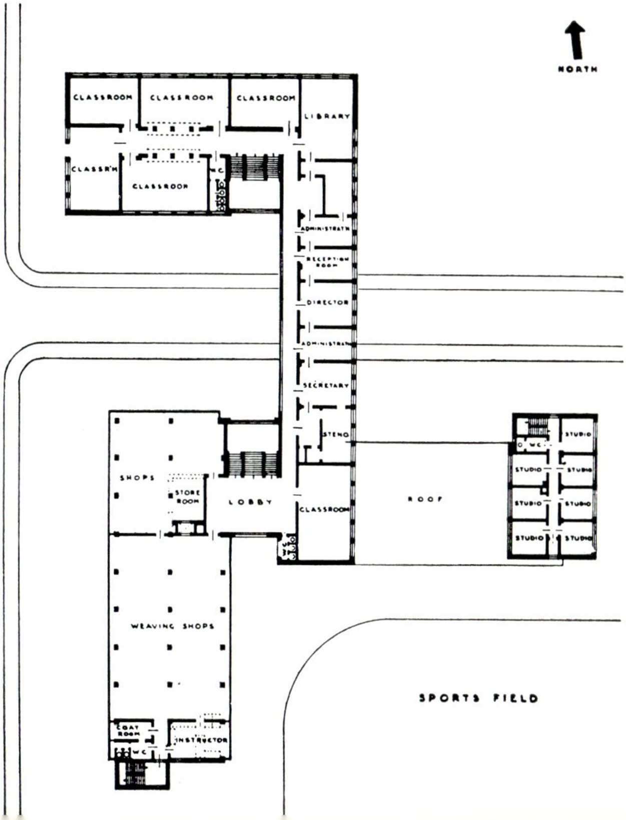
NORTH
CLASSROOM
CLASSROOM
CLASSROOM
LIBRARY
CLASSR'M
CLASSROOM
W.C.
ADMINISTR'N
RECEPTION ROOM
DIRECTOR
ADMINISTR'N
SECRETARY
STENO
SHOPS
STORE ROOM
LOBBY
CLASSROOM
W.C.
ROOF
STUDIO
W.C.
STUDIO
STUDIO
STUDIO
STUDIO
STUDIO
STUDIO
WEAVING SHOPS
COAT ROOM
W.C.
INSTRUCTOR
SPORTS FIELD

This piece of antique formality seems to be some kind of ritual gesture to the ancient gods of order and discipline, for which symmetry is still the most eloquent symbol we have, for the Bauhaus is, above all others, the building in which Gropius dedicated himself and his followers to the concept of the disciplined service of a functional order, and proved the concept to be as expressive and architectural as any exercise in architecture or expression for their own sakes. It is a shrine to the belief that the Machine Age is good.

Crown Hall, Chicago
Mies van der Rohe

Mies van der Rohe's great scheme for the campus buildings at Illinois Institute of Technology seems doomed to remain an unfinished fragment. Barely half a dozen buildings are to his design and close enough together to reveal his original intention of an area planned and buildings built on a common grid of twelve-foot squares. Even so, there are one or two places where one walks out of one building, across a path, and into another with the feeling, not that one is traversing dead ground between separate structures, but merely an unroofed part of a continuous structure. This idea of a continuous structural space, roofed or unroofed, walled or unwalled, at will, has a respectable ancestry in the Modern Movement, but normally presupposes a given structural grid over the whole site before functional subdivision begins. Mies at I I T has followed the more ambiguous (but also more practicable) approach of keeping the pre-existing grid in his head, and filling it out piecemeal with separate buildings that could equally well exist outside this specialised context.

Mies intended to vary this regular built/unbuilt space at certain points by buildings that did not so much contribute to the spatial system as float in pools of space within it. You can hardly

Crown Hall, entrance.

sense this, as the scheme was left at the time of his retirement, because only part of the enclosure of just one pool exists; yet within it, raised by the height of a half-basement and differentiated from his other buildings by a larger scale in all its parts, floats Crown Hall, his masterpiece, the holy of holies, the architecture school.

Effectively, it is a single room, big enough to contain the entire school, and free of columns because the structure is carried in giant trusses clear over the roof, which is hung from them. Entry is by a flight of steps placed classically and symmetrically in the centre of each long side, and all necessary interruptions of the continuous space are grouped closely about the central axis that connects the doors. There are no other permanent subdivisions, and the few there are never rise much above man-high, so that one has, from all parts, an uninterrupted view of the high continuous ceiling, and thus an overwhelming sense of the sheer size of the room and—*via* the all-glass walls above eye-level—of its continuity with the world-space outside.

The idea of placing the whole school in a single continuous space has caused alarm in some quarters (one might do better to cavil at the way the Industrial Design department has been crammed into the basement) but the alarm only shows how ignorant we are of the performance of buildings of this scale and type. The lack of obvious acoustic and visual privacy is a matter of complete indifference in this enormous room—because it is enormous. No one is conspicuous, because his activities are insignificant in comparison with the room and the visible world outside. But because the world (or, at least, the sky) outside is visible all round, it is not distracting—anyone who can read in the park can work in here. And because the nearest sound-reflecting surface is usually the ceiling eighteen feet above (and that is sound absorbing, anyhow) private conversations are not immediately bounced back at one's neighbours and eavesdroppers, and may be effectively inaudible three desks away. Inhabited by serious-minded near-adults, not screaming teenagers, Crown Hall is a crystal casket of meditative calm.

It is also an object lesson in how to be a modern architect. Mies's chosen means of expression are sheets of glass and steel I-beams. Materials that ought to be the commonest stock-in-trade of a Machine-Age architecture: glass because it is the ultimate controller of weather, excluding everything but light, a fine membrane between two climates, one hostile and uncontrolled, the other man-made and adjustable; the steel I-beams because they approximate most closely to the ideal of a non-

Interior in normal use.

existent structure, no other material having such a spectacular ratio between reliable strength and visible substance. With these materials Mies creates a functional space that is orderly, but with such ideal simplicity that order is made manifest only by the structure—floor, upright stanchions, roof—because there is nothing else to see. And because there is nothing else to see but a great space, visual attention, when it shifts from sheer space to smaller things, can only fix on the details. These are few, and almost all of them are concerned with the problem of mating glass to I-beams, the precise collocation of subsidiary metal sections that secures the glass, weatherproof, to the edge of the steel. This simple working detail has been half of Mies's architecture ever since he began to build in steel and glass in America, and he has not solved it yet.

Not because his joints don't work, but simply because he has not yet found the final and perfect joint. He never will, of course. He is human, and may think of a better architecture tomorrow; also, he lives in a most sophisticated technological culture, which may offer him a better component tomorrow. This is the splendour and the misery of modern architecture, for whether or not the architect believes in perfect, ultimate solutions, he still feels the moral obligation to work his brain to the bone producing best-possible solutions for today, which may be superseded with the first post tomorrow. Mies is not the only modern architect to quote 'God is in the details', and it is in details such as those of Crown Hall, perfected today but perfectible tomorrow, that one sees what kind of God is modern architecture's.

Detail of roof truss and wall. Facing page: the Miesian ideal of simplicity, inside and outside the entrance of Crown Hall.

155

INDEX

A

Aalto, Alvar 32, 124-128 (biographical note on 126)
Alford, David and Henderson, Brian 117
Amsterdam; flats in Zaanstraat 53-56
Architects Co-Partnership 62 (note)
Aurora, Illinois; Ford House 64-67

B

Barr, Alfred H. 34
Beardsley, Aubrey 15
Behrens, Peter 16, 31
Bel Geddes, Norman 90
Berg, Max 42
Berlin; Turbine Factory 31
    Liebknecht-Luxemburg Monument 34
Blumberg; Factory 62-64
Boccioni, Umberto 46
Breslau; *Jahrhunderthalle* 42
Brasilia 36, 136-142
Breuer, Marcel 28
Brynmawr; factory 62-63
Bunshaft, Gordon 37, 96-100 (biographical note on 98)

C

Candela, Felix 36, 42-44
Chairs 28
Chandigarh; Capitol 140-142
Chicago; Crown Hall 150-155
    Monadnock Block 42
    Robie House 82-85
di Chirico, Giorgio 106
C.I.A.M. 16-18
Citrohan House 23

Como; Asilo Sant'Elia 78, 79
    Casa del Fascio 77
    Casa Giuliani-Frigerio 79
    Monument 76
    Novocomum 77
le Corbusier 9, 16, 17, 19, 22-27, 33, 35-36, 40, 92-96, 108-112, 140-142 (biographical note on 94)
Costa, Lucio 36, 112, 136-142 (biographical note on 138)

D

Dessau; Bauhaus buildings 146-150
Dorfles, Gillo 36
Dudok, W. M. 39 (with biographical note)

E

Eames, Charles 28, 64
Earl, Harley 114
Eiermann, Egon 62-64
Erskine, Ralph 124

F

Fangio, J. M. 9
Fox River, Illinois; Farnsworth House 49-50
Freyssinet, Eugène 38
Fuller, R. Buckminster 18, 43, 46-47, 118 (biographical note)- 120

G

Gardella, Ignazio 82
Garkau; farm 32
Gatwick; airport buildings 116-119
Giedion, Sigfried 39
Glasgow; school of art 13-15

157

Goff, Bruce 64-66 (biographical note)
Gropius, Walter 16, 146-150 (biographical note on 148)

H
Haering, Hugo 32
Ham Common; S P A N housing 58
Hammond, Peter 27 (note)
Hennebique, François 42
Hilversum; town hall 39
Huis ter Heide; house 84, 85

I
Imatra; Vuoksenniska church 124-128

J
Jacobsen, Arne 124
Johnson, Philip 96-100 (biographical note on 98)

K
Kahn, Albert 62 (note)
Kahn, Louis 72-73 (with biographical note)
de Klerk, Michel 53 (with biographical note)
Kurashiki; town hall 70-73

L
Lasdun, Denys 58-61 (biographical note on 60)
Loewy, Raymond 90
London; cluster block, Bethnal Green 58-59
   Crystal Palace 39, 50-51
   Festival Hall 58
   flats in St James's 58-61
   Highpoint, Highgate 128-132
   penguin pool at Zoo 68-69
   Roehampton development 132
   St Paul's, Bow Common 27
Loos, Adolf 31, 40
Lubetkin, Berthold 68 (with biographical note), 128-132
Luckenwalde; factory 32
Lulea; shopping centre 124

Lynn, Jack; Smith, Ivor and Nicklin, Frederick 134
Lyons, Eric 58

M
Mackintosh, Charles Rennie 13-15 (biographical note on 14)
Maekawa, Kunio 122-124 (biographical note)
Maillart, Robert 40
Maguire, Robert 27
Marinetti, F. T. 40
Marseilles; Unité d'Habitation 92-96
Mathes; holiday house 35
Matté-Trucco, G. 40
Mendelsohn, Eric 32, 84-88 (biographical note on 86)
Mexico City; University Cosmic ray pavilion 42
Mies van der Rohe, Ludwig 9, 16, 28, 34, 96-100 (biographical note on 98), 150-155
Milan; cardboard domes, 43
   C.L.A.S.P. school 142-147
   Pirelli building 100-105
Modulor 26
Moholy-Nagy, Laszlo 26 (and biographical note)
Montuori, Eugenio 104-107
Moretti, Luigi 80-81
Murphy and Mackey 118-120
Muthesius, Hermann 16

N
Nervi, Pierluigi 36, 100-104 (biographical note on 102)
New York; Guggenheim Museum 48
   Lever House 96-100, 112
   Pepsi-Cola building 37
   Racquet Club 96
   Seagram building 96-100
   U N Secretariat 96, 112
Niemeyer, Oscar 36, 136-140 (biographical note on 138)

O
Orly; airship hangars 38
Ornament and Crime 31
Oud, J. J. P. 34 (with biographical note), 54

P
Paris; Eiffel Tower 39, 51-52
   Garage Ponthieu 31
   house in Rue Franklin 42-43
   Pavillon Suisse 108-113
   Villa Cook 34
Perret, Auguste 31, 38, 42
Pevsner, Nikolaus 15
Philadelphia; laboratories 72-75
Picasso, Pablo 10, 46
Poelzig, Hans 32
Poissy; Villa Savoie 23-25, 47-48
Ponti, Gio 9, 100-104 (biographical note on 102)
Posen; water tower 32
Preston; housing 58

R
Racine, Wisconsin; Johnson Wax Co. buildings 86-91
Rietveld, Gerrit T. 28, 56 (with biographical note)
Rio de Janeiro; Ministry of Education 36, 112, 138
Rodovre; town hall 124
Rome; Casa del Girasole 80-81
   Termini Station 104-107
   Terza Roma 104, 106
Ronchamp; pilgrimage chapel of Notre Dame du Haut 27
Ruskin, John 9, 15

S
Saarinen, Eero 112 (biographical note)-116
Sakakura, Junzo 70
Saint Louis, Missouri; Climatron 20, 118-121
Sant'Elia, Antonio 33
Säynätsalo; civic centre 32

Schein, Ionel 44
Schwandbach; bridge 41
Scott, Geoffrey 10
Semper, Gottfried 15
Sheffield; Park Hill 132-136
Skidmore, Owings and Merrill 37, 96-100
Stam, Mart 28
Stirling, James and Gowan, James 58
Stone, Edward D. 18
Stuttgart: Schocken Store 84-88
   Weissenhof Exhibition 34-35
Sydney, N.S.W.; Opera House 124

T
Tange, Kenzo 70 (biographical note)-72
Terragni, Giuseppe 76 (biographical note)-78
Tokyo; Harumi apartment block 122-124
Turin; Fiat factory 41

U
Utrecht; Schröder house 56-58
Utzon, Jörn 124

V
van t'Hoff, Rob 84
Venice; house on the Zattere 81-82
Viollet-le-Duc, E-E 15

W
Warren, Michigan; General Motors Technical Centre 112-116
Williams, Sir Owen 40, 62 (note)
Womersley, J. L. 132
Wright, Frank Lloyd 9, 16 (note), 48, 82 (biographical note)-84, 88-91

Y
Yorke, Rosenberg and Mardall 116-118